DATE DUE

MAR 6 1995	

DEMCO

OCT 2 3 '92

Lewis Howard Latimer

PIONEERS in CHANGE

Lewis Howard Latimer

GLENNETTE TILLEY TURNER

Silver Burdett Press
Englewood Cliffs, New Jer

Dedicated to Winifred Latimer Norman, Gerald Latimer Norman, and Marilyn Kyles.

CONSULTANTS:

Catherine J. Lenix-Hooker
Deputy Chief
Schomburg Center for Research in Black Culture
New York Public Library
New York City

Dr. Elysa E. Robinson
COMPACT Coordinator
Detroit Public Schools
Detroit, Michigan

Acknowledgments, Text Permissions, and Photograph Credits are listed on page 127.

SERIES AND COVER DESIGN:
R STUDIO T• Raúl Rodríguez and Rebecca Tachna

ART DIRECTOR:
Linda Huber

MANAGING EDITOR:
Nancy Furstinger

PROJECT EDITOR:
Richard G. Gallin

PHOTO RESEARCH:
Omni-Photo Communications, Inc.

Published by Silver Burdett Press, Inc., a division of
Simon & Schuster, Inc., Englewood Cliffs, NJ 07632

Library of Congress Cataloging-in-Publication Data
Turner, Glennette Tilley.
Lewis Howard Latimer / Glennette Tilley Turner.
p.   cm.—(Pioneers in change)
Includes bibliographical references and index.
Summary: A biography of the Afro-American inventor who, among other
contributions, invented an inexpensive method for manufacturing carbon filaments
for electric light bulbs.
1. Latimer, Lewis Howard, 1848-1928—Juvenile literature.   2. Inventors—United
States—Biography—Juvenile literature.
3. Afro-American inventors—United States—Biography—Juvenile literature.
[1. Latimer, Lewis Howard, 1848-1928.   2. Inventors.
3. Afro-Americans—Biography.]
I. Title.   II. Series.
T40.L37T87   1990
621.32'6'092—dc20
[B]   90-36264
[92]   CIP
                                                                       AC
Manufactured in the United States of America.
ISBN 0-382-09524-3 [lib. bdg.]
10 9 8 7 6 5 4 3 2 1
ISBN 0-382-24162-2 [pbk.]
10 9 8 7 6 5 4 3 2 1

CONTENTS

1

An Unexpected Welcome

Lewis Howard Latimer's childhood experiences were very different from those of many children growing up in the Boston area during the mid-1850s. Events that had taken place years before Lewis's birth on September 4, 1848, helped to determine the kind of childhood he would have.

Both of Lewis's parents had been slaves in Norfolk, Virginia. The adventures they had during their escape from slavery and after they arrived in Massachusetts is a story in itself. Lewis Latimer's father, George W. Latimer, was the son of Mitchell Latimer. Mitchell Latimer was the brother of the man who owned George's mother, Margaret Olmsted. During his childhood, George Latimer had been a house servant. He was later hired out to do various jobs that included caring for horses, being a laborer, and working as a store clerk. Although George Latimer got to do many different kinds of jobs, there was one thing that never changed: He was always badly treated. Once he was even thrown into jail for his master's debts. For as long as he could remember, George Latimer had always wanted to escape from slavery. As an adult looking back on his early life, he said, "I have thought frequently of running away even when I was a little boy."

Very little is known about Lewis Latimer's mother, Rebecca Smith Latimer. A slaveholder named Mary D. Sayer claimed to own Rebecca, but George Latimer said his wife had been owned by a Mr. DeLacy.

George and Rebecca were married in either January or February 1842. Because they were slaves, however, they could not set up a home and live together as a married couple. Instead, George Latimer had to be content with visiting his wife whenever his owner allowed him to do so. On these visits, George had to be back at work well before sunrise. This was only one of the rules he had to obey if he wanted to see Rebecca. Even after he had followed all the rules, George was once severely beaten by his owner, a storekeeper by the name of James B. Gray. Bitter experience had taught George and Rebecca Latimer that their situation wasn't likely to improve. They therefore decided to take their lives into their own hands. On October 4, 1842, they made a daring escape.

This wasn't the first time George Latimer had tried to escape from slavery. He had run away about two years earlier, but he had been captured. This time he was determined to succeed because his wife was expecting a baby. George and Rebecca Latimer wanted their child to be born in a free state—a state in which there was no slavery. Unless they managed to escape to such a state, their child would be born a slave. A slave child could be taken from his or her parents and sold at the whim of a slaveholder. If this happened, George and Rebecca Latimer might never see their child again.

George and Rebecca Latimer's escape was filled with many suspenseful moments. They boarded a ship in Norfolk and spent the first part of the trip hidden under the forepeak of the vessel. For nine hours they had to lie on stone ballast—the weight that helped to stabilize the ship. Even though they were concealed in darkness, George and Rebecca Latimer were never far from danger. If either of them had sneezed or accidentally made the slightest noise, their escape would have been foiled.

George Latimer later described this frightening experience.

[W]e could peek through the cracks of the partition into the barroom of the vessel, where men who would have gladly captured us were drinking....When we went aboard the vessel at Frenchtown a man stood in the gangway who was a wholesaler of liquors. He knew me, for my master kept a saloon and was his customer. But I pulled my Quaker hat over my eyes and passed him unrecognized. I had purchased a first-class passage and at once went into the cabin and stayed there. Fortunately he did not enter.

Between Baltimore, Maryland (a slave state), and Philadelphia, Pennsylvania (a free state), George pretended to be a gentleman slaveholder and Rebecca pretended to be his servant. Once they reached the North, they traveled as husband and wife.

Daring and ingenuity paid off. On October 8, 1842, the Latimers arrived in the free state of Massachusetts four days after they had left Virginia. They knew that because they were fugitive slaves—runaways—they would be in constant danger of being captured and forced back into slavery. It wasn't long before their fears seemed to come true.

On the day the Latimers set foot in Boston, George was recognized by someone. William Carpenter was the person who spotted George Latimer. Carpenter had worked for Latimer's owner, James B. Gray. He contacted Gray in Norfolk. On October 15, this ad appeared in the Norfolk *Beacon*, a Virginia newspaper:

> Ran away on Monday night last, my Negro man called George Latimer. He is about five feet three or four inches high, about twenty-two years of age, his complexion is bright yellow, is of a compact, well-made frame, and is rather silent and slow-spoken.

Mary D. Sayer, Rebecca Latimer's owner, placed this ad in the *American Beacon*:

> Ran away from the subscriber [Sayer] last evening, Negro woman Rebecca in company (as is supposed) with her husband George Latimer, belonging to James B. Gray of this place. She is twenty years of age, dark mulatto, copper colored, good co[u]ntenance [appearance and behavior toward others], bland voice, and self-possessed and easy in her manners when addressed. She was married February last [1842], and is at this time obviously [expecting a baby].
>
> She will in all probability endeav[o]r [most likely try] to reach some of the free states.
>
> All persons are hereby cautioned against harboring [giving shelter and protection to] said slave, and masters of vessels from carrying her from this port....[R]eward will be paid upon delivery.
>
> Mary D. Sayer

James B. Gray arrived in Boston on October 18, 1842, and had George Latimer arrested. The Boston police did this without a warrant—a legal document giving them the right to make the arrest. They also imprisoned Latimer without bringing any legal charges against him. The behavior of the police officers was clearly against the law. Latimer was held in the Leverett Street Jail. News of the incident spread rapidly. Many people were outraged at the manner in which George Latimer had been arrested. Gray hired Elbridge Gerry Austin as his lawyer when public protest began to grow. News of the arrest spread quickly. Soon Latimer had Amos B. Merrill, Charles M. Ellis, and Samuel E. Sewall as his lawyers.

The day after Latimer's arrest, nearly 300 African-American men assembled around the courthouse to prevent Gray from taking Latimer out of the city illegally. On Sunday, October 30, a spirited public meeting was held at the famous Faneuil Hall in Boston.

Public announcements of this meeting had run in all the Boston newspapers. It brought out a cross-section of people. Some were against slavery, others were for it, and some were just curious. One of Latimer's lawyers, Samuel E. Sewall, presided. He had been an abolitionist—a person working to end slavery— for many years and was a founder of the New England Antislavery Society in 1831. Three men—one of whom was Charles Lenox Redmond, a noted black orator—were appointed secretaries. The chairman made a statement about George Latimer's case. Following this, eighteen resolutions were read. One stated, "That in the person of George Latimer, now confined in Leverett Street jail on the charge of being a slave, are embodied the rights and immunities of all people...."

Faneuil Hall was an ideal place to protest the jailing of George Latimer. During the American Revolution, many town meetings had been held there to protest British rule. John Adams—who would become the second president of the United States—called the building in which the hall was

George Latimer gained instant fame in Boston when slave catchers tried to take him back to Virginia.

located the Cradle of Liberty. The hall was famous for another reason. During the Boston Massacre in 1770, it was there that another fugitive slave, Crispus Attucks, became the first man to die for America's independence from Great Britain.

Protest meetings were also held in many other Massachusetts towns: Salem, Springfield, Lynn, New Bedford, Abingdon, Sherburne, Worcester, and Northampton. At each gathering, speakers tried to rally the public to support Latimer's cause. The "singing Hutchinsons"—direct descendants of the first governor of Massachusetts—appealed to audiences with such songs as "Liberate the Bondsman." The poet John Greenleaf Whittier immortalized the *Latimer* case in his poem "Virginia to Massachusetts."

Other abolitionists became involved in trying to get Latimer released. William Lloyd Garrison published news of the case in his newspaper, *The Liberator*. Frederick Douglass, an eloquent speaker and a leading abolitionist who had himself escaped from slavery only four years earlier, wrote a letter to Garrison about his efforts to raise money to purchase Latimer's freedom. Garrison printed this letter in his paper. This was the first time Douglass's writings had ever been published. He later went on to write books and to edit his own newspaper. Three other men—Dr. Henry Bowditch, William Francis Channing, and Frederick Cabot—started a newspaper called the *Latimer Journal and North Star*. It was founded a short time before Latimer was released from slavery. The newspaper came out three times a week. Only a few issues were printed, but they contained firsthand accounts. One issue of the journal carried a long interview with George Latimer himself. Latimer described what would happen if he had to return to slavery. "I expect if

Frederick Douglass, one of the leading abolitionists, had escaped from slavery in 1838, four years before George and Mary Latimer escaped.

I was carried back to be beaten and whipped 39 lashes, and perhaps to be washed in pickle afterwards."

The week before Latimer was released was a tense one. There were rumors that a warship was being held in readiness to take Latimer back to Norfolk. Another rumor declared that the ship's captain would refuse to take Latimer back. The situation was constantly changing. Chief Justice Lemuel Shaw of the Massachusetts Supreme Court issued a ruling that gave Gary the right to claim Latimer as his personal property. Meanwhile, two petitions had been signed by many abolitionists. In these petitions, the abolitionists requested that Sheriff Eveleth order Cooledge, the deputy keeper of the Suffolk County jail, to free Latimer. Cooledge was also acting as an agent for Gray. The abolitionists threatened to have Cooledge removed from office if he didn't meet their request. Cooledge took the threat seriously. Soon afterward, he told Gray that he would no longer be able to act as his agent.

At the same time, the lawyer Samuel Sewall gave Latimer some advice on what he should do in case Gray tried to take him by force. The advice was simple: Latimer should scream as loud as he could. This would alert the fifteen to twenty black abolitionists who were guarding the jail, and he would be rescued.

Other abolitionists were busy trying to purchase Latimer from Cooledge. One was an African American whose name is unrecorded, perhaps because he was also an escaped slave. The other was Dr. Henry Bowditch. Cooledge's lowest figure was $800, but the African American was able to talk him into accepting $650. Dr. Bowditch agreed to pay it. They set a time for the transaction to take place. Shortly after these negotiations were completed, Dr. Bowditch discovered that the sheriff had issued a new order. It directed

Cooledge to let Latimer go before the day of the hearing. Bowditch knew that there was no place that Gray could keep Latimer that would prevent his being rescued by the men who had been guarding the jail. Bowditch now felt that it was not necessary to pay the $650 if Latimer was about to be set free. A black minister, the Reverend Samuel Caldwell, acting on behalf of some of the members of his church, didn't want to take that chance. According to George Latimer and John W. Hutchinson (one of the family of singers), the Reverend Samuel Caldwell purchased Latimer for $400. J. W. Hutchinson was about to sing at a protest rally when a man ran through the door shouting, "He's free! He's free!" Everyone at the rally was ecstatic.

Exactly one month after he was arrested for being a runaway slave, George Latimer had become a free man. During that month of uncertainty, Rebecca Latimer had been hidden by abolitionists. One report stated that "she was secreted [hidden] at the house of a friendly abolitionist on High Street." Another said that both George and Rebecca Latimer "stayed at the homes of friendly blacks." It is possible that even after George Latimer was released from jail, he and his wife had to move from one location to another to stay out of the reach of slave catchers.

Speaking of his wife during this time, George Latimer later wrote: "Her whereabouts were never disclosed, and her master made no further trouble after I was released." Latimer went on to say that soon after the trial his first child, George, was born on Newhall Street, in Lynn, in the free state of Massachusetts. Some records indicate that the baby was actually born in Lowell, although there is an account of George Latimer, Sr., being in Lynn in November 1842. Samuel Filebee was a Quaker who lived near Newhall Street. He was known for his strong antislavery views and was credited with helping George Latimer. The birth of his child spurred George Latimer, Sr., into action. He and other abolitionists who had worked to get him out of jail were now determined to see new laws passed. These laws would prevent other fugitive slaves from having the kind of experience Latimer had had. He wrote: "Immediately after my release I began to attend anti-slavery conventions and appeal for signatures to the famous 'Latimer' petitions, to be presented to the [Massachusetts State] Legislature and to [the U.S.] Congress." These petitions were known as the Great Petitions. There was almost as much excitement and activity surrounding them as there had been about getting Latimer out of jail.

More than 110,000 people signed these petitions. They were taken to the Massachusetts legislature and to the U.S. Congress. The outcome of this effort was that Massachusetts passed a personal liberty law. This law made it illegal for state officers to help capture fugitive slaves. The bill did not pass in the U.S. Congress, even though it was presented by John Adams's son, Congressman John Quincy Adams, who had previously been the sixth president of the United States.

As disappointed as backers of that federal bill were, the *Latimer* case was still considered a landmark case by American abolitionists. It was the first of several famous fugitive-slave cases that were tried in Boston. The *Latimer* case was also important because it influenced two events that had nationwide impact on pre–Civil War history: the passage of the Fugitive Slave Act in 1850 and the *Dred Scott* decision in 1857. The Fugitive Slave Act was passed by Congress in order to prevent slaves like Latimer from gaining their freedom. It denied jury trials to runaway slaves and provided a reward for each fugitive who was caught. Federal marshals could require ordinary citizens to help enforce the law.

People who violated the law by helping escaped slaves could be fined a thousand dollars and sent to prison for six months.

In the *Dred Scott* decision, the U.S. Supreme Court ruled that a slave who was taken to a free state or territory temporarily did not become a citizen of that territory or state and did not become free. The Fugitive Slave Act and the *Dred Scott* decision made escape far more dangerous. However, these actions sparked a new sense of urgency among slaves and abolitionists. They viewed the Fugitive Slave Act and the *Dred Scott* decision as awesome challenges to be overcome.

Meanwhile, George Latimer was finding that freedom was also an awesome challenge. He and his wife, Rebecca, had taken tremendous risks to escape from slavery. Upon arriving in Boston they did not find the safe haven they had dreamed of. Instead, they were immediately faced with the uncertainties of George's imprisonment and Rebecca's need to find a hiding place in unfamiliar surroundings.

The *Latimer* case had made George Latimer famous, but this fame did little to ease the financial burdens the Latimer family now faced. Latimer was skilled at doing many different kinds of work, and he was now a free man. All the same, he was unable to earn enough money to support his family.

2

Growing Up in Turbulent Times

By the time Lewis Latimer was born on September 4, 1848, the family was living just outside of Boston, in Chelsea, Massachusetts. George and Rebecca Latimer already had two sons, George A. and William H., and a daughter, Margaret.

According to Lewis's journal, which is written as if he were writing about someone else,

> His first recollection of a home was a house on Oswego Street[,] a street which ran east from Harrison Avenue in Boston....Lewis remained here but a short time and then moved a little farther uptown to Orange Lane, a strictly Irish neighborhood.... From Orange Lane the Latimers moved to the west end of Boston near Massachusetts General Hospital and after a short time here, went to live on Phillips St.[,] then known as Southac St., a strictly colored neighborhood. They were located here for a number of years.

The Fugitive Slave Act had passed by the time the Latimer family moved to Phillips Street. Having Lewis and Harriet Hayden for neighbors must have given the family a secure feeling. The Haydens operated an Underground Railroad "station" in their home. The Underground Railroad was a system of cooperation among active antislavery people in the United States. It secretly helped fugitive slaves to reach safe places in the North or in Canada. The Haydens themselves had been helped in their escape from slavery. They helped other runaway slaves by using their house as a hiding place. In 1850, they had hidden yet another couple, William and Ellen Craft. And in 1851, Lewis Hayden and a lawyer rushed into the courthouse and rescued a fugitive named Shadrack.

Even though the Latimers could feel relatively secure, money was so scarce that Lewis could not have had a carefree childhood. He had to go to work as a very young child. His family needed the little money he could earn doing jobs. Some of these jobs gave Lewis a chance to spend long hours at his father's side. And they were the kinds of jobs that let them talk with each other as they worked. Lewis worked at his father's barbership on Cambridge Street.

Later, according to Lewis's journal, his father "worked in a store on Washington Street paper hanging." Young Lewis worked with his father at night and, as he reveals, "in this way became quite expert as a paper hanger."

In addition to helping his father, Lewis had another job—that of selling newspapers. One of these papers was *The Liberator*, which was published by William Lloyd Garrison. Garrison and many other men and women in Massachusetts hated slavery and did everything they could to end it. Before the days of radio and television, newspapers were the most effective way of communicating ideas. Garrison's *Liberator* was filled with articles about the evils of slavery. During George Latimers' jailing, *The Liberator* had kept readers well informed. Now George Latimer's son, Lewis, was selling the newspaper.

When Lewis was ten years old, his father deserted the family. No one knows exactly what drove George Latimer to such a desperate act. His struggles to become a free man probably caused him a great deal of fear and anxiety. On top of this, his family was growing and he could not provide for them. All the attention Latimer received during his arrest and jailing may have led him to believe that surely a black man with skills could make a good life for his family in the Boston area. He may have lost this belief when he realized that many opportunities were denied him even though he was in the North.

Dr. Asa Davis, an authority and expert on the life of George Latimer, has suggested that Latimer may have had another reason for deserting his family: the Fugitive Slave Act of 1850. This law placed former slaves (and even African Americans who had been born in the free Northern states) in constant danger. The Fugitive Slave Act made it legal for slave catchers to roam the Northern states in search of runaway slaves. These slave catchers were only supposed to locate fugitive slaves. In those days, however, a person's "freedom papers" were often the only proof that he or she was free. If the slave catchers destroyed these papers (which had to be carried at all times), that person could be forced into slavery. According to Dr. Asa Davis, George Latimer may have moved about in order to keep from being enslaved again. It is also possible that Latimer thought he would be a particular target for slave catchers since his case had been so well publicized. If slave catchers could have forced him back into slavery, that would have done much more to discourage would-be runaways than the capture of someone less well known.

It is possible that Latimer had lived in constant fear from the time the Fugitive Slave Act became law until he disappeared and that the Dred Scott decision doubled the danger. Perhaps he believed that he and his family were safer if they were not living together. This way he would not put his wife and children in the position of being captured with him. Also, it would be easier and less noticeable for one man to move from place to place than for a family of six.

After studying the life of George Latimer, Davis came to this conclusion: Although Latimer's family did not know where he was, he was usually close by. He would look in on them whenever he could—even though he could not make his presence known or do anything to help them.

While living on Phillips Street, Lewis went to primary school and then to the Phillips Grammar School on Anderson Street. Lewis's school attendance was not very good. School had to be squeezed in between his many jobs. But he loved school. He was a good student. Lewis did so well that he even skipped a grade. His favorite subjects were reading, creative writing, and art. These subjects became lifelong interests of his.

Unfortunately, George Latimer's disappearance put an end to Lewis's school days. Lewis had to leave school and work full-time in order to help his mother. Without her husband, Rebecca Latimer faced very difficult times. She now had to support a family of four children. Lewis Latimer's journal gives details of what took place.

His two brothers were sent to a state institution then known as the Farm School, from where they were bound out [that is, placed in the care of employers who would provide a room and food and perhaps a little pay]. George was [bound out] to a farmer and William to a hotel keeper in Springfield [Massachusetts]. Margaret, the girl, was taken by a friend and Lewis remained in his mother's home until she got a chance to go to sea as a stewardess....[S]he arranged to send him to the Farm School.

Lewis was unhappy at the farm school. Eventually his brother William returned to the school and found him there. William worked out a plan of escape, and soon he, Lewis, and a white friend of theirs managed to get away from the school. It took them several days to make their way back to Boston. They walked, hitched rides on the railroad, and begged for food. Their arrival was a big surprise to their mother and sister, who were now keeping house together.

Once they were back home in Boston, William and Lewis had to find work in order to support themselves. In his journal Lewis explained: "Their mother sheltered them until they could go to work such as boys could do." Lewis waited on tables and did odd jobs at a private home in Roxbury. Soon afterward, he was able to find a job as an office boy at the law offices of Issac Hull Wright. Lewis was only thirteen years old, barely a teenager, but already he had taken on the adult responsibility of earning a living.

By the time Lewis was fifteen, Boston was buzzing with talk of "the War." Wherever people gathered, this was what they talked about. The American Civil War was being fought between the North and the South over the issue of slavery. The Union forces represented the North and fought to end slavery. The Confederate forces fought to defend slavery and their way of life in the South. Hundreds of thousands of soldiers were being killed or wounded. Newspapers reported news of the battles. On September 22, 1862—a few days after the North won the important Battle of Antietam—President Abraham Lincoln issued the Emancipation Proclamation. The final proclamation was signed and went into effect on January 1, 1863. It stated that all persons "held in any state...in rebellion [that is, fighting the Northern forces] shall be...forever free." These words brought new hope to those who wanted to help bring an end to slavery.

Boston Harbor was the center of much activity. Ships were being loaded with war supplies for the Northern troops. Able-bodied men were leaving the safety of Boston to fight in this war. Many former salves saw the war as an opportunity to fight and help see to it that slavery was wiped out once and for all. When President Abraham Lincoln called for troops, 1,500 Massachusetts men responded within four days.

Both of Lewis's brothers joined the Union forces. George enlisted in the Twenty-ninth Connecticut Army Regiment, and William joined the navy. But Lewis wasn't quite old enough to enlist. He soon thought of a way to solve this problem, however. He pretended to be older than he was and joined the navy on September 13, 1864. He became a cabin boy on the U.S.S. *Massasoit*, a side-wheel gunboat. He served under Rear Admiral David D. Porter and Commander Richard T. Renshaw. Lewis saw action on the James River in Virginia, not far from where his parents had lived when they were slaves. The *Massasoit* was part of the North Atlantic Blockading Squadron. The gunboat had now made several escort voyages (in which it protected other ships) from New York to Hampton Roads, Virginia. On January 24, 1865, it took part in the battle with Confederate forces at Howellett's House. During the following months, the ship stood by to prevent any Southern forces from reaching the coast. On April 6, the *Massasoit* was ordered to carry important messages to General William T. Sherman in North Carolina. The ship remained on duty in the Sounds of North Carolina during the last days of the Civil War. At the end of the war, the *Massasoit* returned to Boston. Lewis was honorably discharged from service in the navy on July 3, 1865.

In his journal, which was obviously written after he was an adult, Lewis wrote: "There was none of his [Lewis Latimer's] family in the city at that time, but shortly after his mother appeared and they went into housekeeping in a couple of rooms on Phillips Street."

What Lewis obviously did not realize is that his father had been back in town during the Civil War. He was listed as a paperhanger in the 1863 and 1864 Boston City Directories. He may have left Boston by the time Lewis returned from the war, but was included in the Boston directory in 1868. He lived at 42 W. Orange—and all three of his sons were living at the rear of 69 Phillips Street. Evidently Lewis, George, and William were unaware that their father was back in Boston. This is consistent with Dr. Asa Davis's conclusion that Lewis Latimer's father was usually nearby and that he probably would look in on the family without making his presence known. That city directory did not list women unless they were heads of households. It did not give any clue as to the whereabouts of Lewis's mother or sister in 1868.

Lewis found that in some ways the city of Boston had changed between his childhood days and the post–Civil War period. Many new immigrants—people from other countries—had settled in Boston. Thousands of them were from Ireland. The Irish had left their own country to escape starvation during a serious potato famine. Boston had a special place of honor in many people's hearts. The city was the home of some of the strongest antislavery protests in the country. It therefore celebrated the North's victory in its own special way—with a giant Peace Jubilee. City officials even built a special stadium for the event. The celebration was so noisy that President Ulysses S. Grant was forced to cover his ears.

Lewis thought the Boston he had come home to was very different from the city he had known as a boy. But he soon discovered that some things hadn't changed at all. For example, Lewis found that it was almost as difficult for him to earn enough money to support himself in Boston as it had been for his father to support their family. In his journal, Lewis described how he went from one place to another trying to find work. He said that he couldn't find anything until "finally a colored girl who took care of the office of some lady copyists [there were no typewriters then] was asked to recommend a colored boy as office boy, one 'with a taste for drawing.'" Lewis applied for the job and was hired for three dollars a week. His employer was Crosby and Gould (later known as Crosby and Gregory) at 34 School Street.

Crosby and Gould was a firm of patent lawyers—lawyers who prepared and reviewed patent applications. When an inventor takes out a patent, he or she registers a particular idea or invention with the government. A patent is a government document giving the inventor rights to the invention for a limited time. A patent gives the inventor the right to prevent others from making, using, or selling the invention. Lewis was fascinated by the drawings the drafts-man in the firm prepared for the U.S. Patent Office in Washington, D.C. At that time, he believed that all knowledge was found in books, "so when he saw the man making drawings he watched to find out what tools he used [;] then he went to a secondhand book store and got a book on drawing." [*Note*: Latimer frequently refers to himself in the third person in his journal.]

Latimer saved money to purchase some secondhand drawing tools. Day after day he watched the draftsman at the firm, noting how he used the instruments. Night after night he practiced making drawings until "he felt thoroughly master of them."

One day Latimer asked the draftsman, "May I do some drawings for you?" The draftsman had no idea whether Lewis could do the type of drawings required by the patent office. He laughed at Latimer but eventually gave him a chance to demonstrate what he could do. To his surprise, the draftsman discovered "that Lewis was a real draftsman, so he let him do some of his work from time to time and one day the boss saw him at work and was so pleased that he let him work everyday and gradually raised his wages."

Lewis Latimer worked at Crosby and Gould for eleven years. During that time, he rose from an office boy who earned three dollars a week to become the firm's chief draftsman. His earnings were now twenty dollars a week. (Although the other draftsman had received five dollars more for the same work, twenty dollars was still a good wage in those days.) Latimer became so skilled that it became his job to supervise the construction of the working models of inventions that were required by the U.S. Patent Office at that time. Eventually he was put in charge of the business when George Wilson Gregory, his employer, was away from the office.

These were happy times for Lewis Latimer. Things were going well at work, and he had met and fallen in love

This is an early photograph of Mary Wilson Latimer, wife of Lewis Howard Latimer. They were married in 1873.

with Mary Wilson of Fall River, Massachusetts. The couple were married on November 10, 1873. Latimer's journal does not reveal the personal side of his life. It does not describe how or where or when Lewis and Mary met. Her hometown of Fall River is a seaport about fifty miles from Boston. It was best known as being one of the largest cotton cloth manufacturing centers in the world. The Fall River area was in its heyday after the Civil War. Ships and railroad lines transported the cloth to New York City and Boston and beyond.

How Mary Wilson's family fit into the scheme of things in Fall River is not known. What is known from a journal that Mary kept is that she wrote and expressed herself like a very intelligent and well-educated person. It is unclear whether she had been self-educated as Lewis had been or had had an opportunity to stay in school longer than he did. What is known from the poetry that Lewis wrote is that he and Mary shared many interests and were a very happy couple. One of the things that contributed to their happiness is that Mary appreciated and encouraged her husband's efforts to learn all that he could about his work.

Working in a patent lawyer's office had allowed Lewis to gain firsthand knowledge of how inventions were patented. He soon realized that he had some ideas of his own that he wanted to develop. In 1874, Lewis Latimer received his first patent. He and W. C. Brown became co-inventors of an improvement on the water closet, or bathroom, that was used on trains. Lewis Latimer had taken his first step as an inventor and a pioneer in changing the way people lived.

3

A New World Takes Shape

Soon after getting his first patent, Lewis Latimer met a teacher at a school for the deaf located near his office. The teacher was Alexander Graham Bell. Bell's father, Alexander Melville Bell, was the inventor of a method called Visible Speech, which enabled deaf people to talk with each other. He had created a Visible Speech alphabet with a symbol for every sound the vocal cords could produce. Alexander Graham Bell taught his father's method at the school. His interests in sound led him to invent a machine that he hoped would make it possible for a human voice to be carried through wires for long distances. He wanted to get a patent on this device. He believed his invention would make it possible for deaf people to hear speech. He was especially motivated because both his mother and his wife-to-be were deaf.

When Bell learned that Latimer was a draftsman, he asked Latimer to draw up the plans for the invention. Although the two men worked within a block of each other, the difference in their schedules made it difficult for them to get together. Bell taught day and evening classes. Latimer later wrote: "I was obliged to stay at the office until after nine P.M. when he was free from his night classes, to get my instructions from him, as to how I was to make the drawings for the application for a patent upon the telephone." Latimer was no stranger to hard work, however, and he completed the design for Bell.

On February 14, 1876, Bell filed an application with the U.S. Patent Office for the device we know today as the telephone. The patent was granted on March 7, 1876.

Some scholars believe that Latimer also helped Bell with the wording of the telephone patent application. Latimer would certainly have been an excellent resource person. He had recently gotten a patent, and the Crosby and Gregory firm specialized in processing and reviewing patent applications. Although at that time Latimer had not yet worked with many electrical devices, he was certainly knowledgeable about patent requirements.

Bell and Latimer were similar in the way both approached learning about new things. Each man believed if he wanted to learn how to do something, he could learn it— if he invested enough time and effort. That's how Latimer learned drafting well enough to become chief draftsman. And that's how Bell learned enough about electricity to develop the telephone. He had wanted to apply his knowledge of Visible Speech to the invention of the telephone. But he lacked the electrical knowledge to develop his ideas. Bell was discussing his thoughts with Professor Joseph Henry, who was an expert on sound transmission. When Bell said he didn't have electrical knowledge, the professor said, "Get it!" And Bell did.

The result of the cooperative effort between Alexander

Graham Bell and Lewis Howard Latimer was more far-reaching than either man could have imagined. Neither of them suspected that this single invention would lead to a worldwide communications network—one that people, governments, and businesses now depend on so completely that it is impossible to imagine life without it. The telephone revolutionized the way people lived and worked.

Drawing the plans for the world's first telephone gave Latimer one of his first opportunities to work with an electrical device. He began the "Electrical Recollections" section of his journal by describing his association with Bell. Until he met Bell, Latimer's only opportunity to do this kind of work had been the drawings he made for electrical railroad signals at Crosby and Gould.

Two years after drawing the plans for the telephone, Latimer was employed by Joseph Adams, another patent lawyer who was also located on School Street. Latimer's responsibilities there were similar to those he had had at his former place of employment. When this work ended, he took a job in the pattern shop at the Esterbrook Iron Foundry in South Boston. This job was short-lived, however. In 1879 Latimer found himself out of work. At the end of the year, he and his wife moved from Boston to Bridgeport, Connecticut, where his sister, Margaret Hawley, now lived with her husband.

Bridgeport was booming at this time. This came as a surprise to Latimer, even though he had seen many tall chimneys from the boat as it approached the city's harbor. A newspaper article dated February 15, 1880, quoted him as saying, "It was hardly to be supposed that a city so near New York could possess much life of its own." Latimer soon discovered that Bridgeport was an important industrial center. Some of the items produced there had a worldwide reputation. The city was the home of the Wheeler and Wilson and Howe sewing machines, and of a "Glove Fitting Corset" company. In his journal, Latimer went on to report: "The place is perfectly alive with inventors and it would be next to impossible to throw a stone into any company of men gathered anywhere about in the street without hitting one." For example, one of the better-known inventors living in Bridgeport at this time was Henry House. He had developed a twelve-horsepower steam automobile and a car heater many years before the days of the Model-T Ford.

Although Bridgeport had many industries, Latimer was forced to take up his old trade of paperhanging when he arrived there. After a while, however, he was able to locate a drafting job. He was asked to make a small drawing for the Follansbee Machine shop. While Latimer was working on this drawing, Hiram S. Maxim—founder of and chief electrician for the U. S. Electric Lighting Company, and also an inventor—walked into the machine shop.

Maxim said, "Hello, I never saw a colored man making drawings—where did you learn?" Maxim was as surprised to see Latimer's ability as the draftsman at Crosby and Gould had been. He didn't realize that if someone really wants to learn something, he or she can do it—even without formal schooling.

Latimer told Maxim where he had learned drafting. It turned out that at one time Maxim had worked for the same company. Crosby and Gould had an excellent reputation, so Maxim knew that Latimer must be a first-rate draftsman. Maxim immediately hired Latimer to be his assistant manager and draftsman.

Maxim had reached a high point in his career. Electric lighting was so new that many people had not yet seen it. Maxim was giving dazzling demonstrations of this new source of light. One night he entertained members of the Bridgeport Scientific Society at the opera house with a display of the "wondrous brightness of the electric light."

While working for Maxim, Latimer learned everything that was known about the brand-new field of electric lighting. Thomas Alva Edison had patented the electric light only a year before Latimer went to work for Maxim. The light consisted of a glass bulb with a wire filament inside. The carbon filaments were made of such materials as bamboo, paper, or thread. They were made by burning cellulose found in those materials inside a bulb from which almost all air had been removed. In such a vacuum—without air—the cellulose breaks down and leaves a carbon "skeleton." This "skeleton" serves as the filament in an electric light. When an electric current is sent through a wire into the vacuum of the bulb, it causes the filament to become hot enough to glow.

The electric light brought about dramatic changes. People were no longer limited to candles, gas or oil lamps, or the sun as sources of light. The very idea of having an unflickering light to read or work by was a turning point in human history. Still, it was not yet practical to install electric lights in homes. The reason was simple: These bulbs burned out much too quickly. They lasted only a few days. If only a long-burning filament could be found, electric lights could brighten homes all over the world!

Many electric companies sprang up. They hoped to make bundles of money from this exciting new invention. But first, someone had to discover the secret of a filament that would allow the light to burn for many hours. It was too expensive to constantly replace burnt-out light bulbs. So the race was on—not only in the United States, but also in England, Russia, and elsewhere. Electric companies everywhere were frantically searching for a way to make a long-lasting filament. They believed that the first company to find a solution would make a fortune.

Men who had distinguished themselves in the new field of electric lighting were conducting extensive research. The list included Thomas Alva Edison and Hiram S. Maxim in the United States, Frederick de Moleyns and Sir Joseph Wilson Swan in England, and Alexandre de Lodyguine in Russia. While these men busied themselves in a frenzy of discovery, Lewis Latimer quietly mastered the fine points of electric lighting. He painstakingly conducted one experiment after another. Was it possible that this self-taught son of slaves would be the person to single-handedly invent an inexpensive, long-lasting filament?

CHAPTER

4

Latimer Unlocks the Secret

AfterAfter making hundreds of attempts, Lewis Latimer finally succeeded in unlocking the secret of the light bulb as we know it today. He was the person who found what almost everyone in the electrical industry had been searching for—a successful method of producing longer-lasting, less expensive carbon filaments.

Many of the books and articles written about the birth of the electrical industry fail to give Latimer credit for his breakthrough. There are two possible explanations for this. The first is that the contribution of an individual inventor was often credited to his employer. The second explanation is that Latimer was an African American living at a time when the achievements of African Americans were not highly publicized. His invention did not receive the attention it deserved. On the other hand, Edison developed many inventions, and when people heard his name, they usually thought of electric lighting. Most people therefore assumed that Edison—rather than Latimer—was the inventor of the inexpensive method of manufacturing carbon filaments. There are many documents to prove that Latimer was in fact the person who invented this process. Without it, the electric light industry could not have moved forward to become what it is today.

Latimer's method involved putting blanks (or shapes) of fibrous materials (such as paper or strips of wood) into small cardboard envelopes. These "stuffed envelopes" were then exposed to high temperatures under airless conditions. Latimer kept the blanks from sticking to the envelope in either of two ways:

1. By coating the blanks or the inside of the envelope with a nonsticky substance or

2. By putting the blanks between two strips of tissue paper.

The method that had been used before Latimer's invention often resulted in carbons being broken or becoming irregular in shape. The unique feature of Latimer's invention was that it enclosed the blanks in cardboard. The cardboard expanded and contracted at the same rate as the paper or wood from which the blanks were made.

Latimer's invention had great significance. It meant that electric light would now be both practical and more affordable. Carbon filaments could be produced for less money, and they would last longer than earlier versions had. Most important, Latimer's invention now made it possible for electric lights to be installed in homes. Children who had done their homework by lamplight could now have bright, steady illumination from an electric bulb. Family members could enjoy reading the Bible or the newspaper in the evenings. Parents could read stories to their children at bedtime. The benefits were numerous, and they weren't

The Latimer light bulb and light socket.

limited to homes. With Latimer's invention, even small businesses could now afford to have electric light.

Latimer applied for this patent—"The Process for Manufacturing Carbons"—on February 19, 1881. Almost a year passed between the time he filed the application and the time he received it. Finally, on January 17, 1882, Latimer was granted the patent that would mean so much to the new electrical industry. At the time he made the invention, Latimer was working for the U.S. Electric Lighting Company. He was expected to assign this patent to the company rather then claim credit for it himself. He did. The result was that the profits went to the company rather than to the inventor.

Lewis Latimer was a spirited, energetic man—he wasn't one to drag his feet. While waiting for the patent on carbon filaments, he went on to make other contributions. In September 1881, Lewis H. Latimer and Joseph V. Nichols received a patent for an improved incandescent electric lamp. With this development, the two inventors found a better method of connecting the carbon filament to the lead wires at the base of a lamp. Hiram S. Maxim, who was still Latimer's employer, named this lamp the "Maxim electric lamp."

This wasn't the first time Maxim had taken credit for someone else's work. Professor William Sawyer, an inventor who had once worked with Maxim, told a newspaper reporter: "I know Mr. Maxim very well, and while he is beyond doubt one of the best mechanical engineers in this country, I have no hesitation in saying that in his last attempt at electric lighting he has made a wholesale appropriation [taking or making use of without permission] of other people's property." Sawyer made these comments during an interview in which he stated his belief that Maxim had infringed on—made use of without permission—some of Edison's patents. Sawyer didn't like Edison. But he did say of him, "I have respect for a man that travels on his own merits." This was very different from his views on Maxim. Sawyer also said that he "did not like Maxim and was distrustful of him: several times he had the effrontery [shameless boldness] to claim to others before my face ideas given by me."

Not surprisingly, Latimer's carbon filaments were first used in the "Maxim lamp." The filaments could be made into any shape, so—as might be expected—Maxim produced M-shaped filaments. (There is no record that Maxim offered to make them in an L shape for "Latimer.") There was no doubt that Maxim had a tendency not to give credit where credit was due. But Latimer continued to work for him and to develop new methods and equipment for the lighting industry. It wasn't long before he recognized the value of wiring streetlamps in parallel circuits. The first electric street lamps had been wired in series. With series wiring, all the lights went out if any single one failed and went out. With a parallel circuit, if one light goes out, all the other lights continue to burn.

The electrical industry was still so new that there were many problems to be solved. In his journal, Latimer wrote: "Electrical measurement had not then been invented and all our work was by guess." For example, the only kind of electrical wire that was on the market then was lightweight bell wire. Its use often resulted in dangerous heating, and even fire in some instances. When proper wire size standards were developed, electrical installations became much safer.

During the early 1880s, both incandescent and arc lamps were in use. Several months after patenting his process for manufacturing carbon filaments, Lewis Latimer and John Tregoning received a patent for what they called a Globe Supporter. The device was actually a base for electric arc lamps. Like Latimer's patent for carbon filaments, however, this invention was also assigned to the U.S. Electric Lighting Company.

Arc lamps worked on a principle that was very different from that of incandescent lamps. Instead of having a single filament, arc lights had two upright rods of carbon with a gap between them. Electrical current was sent through the rods, and the current jumped the gap. This produced a very bright but noisy light. These bright, noisy lights were used to light city streets and railroad stations. Long after they were no longer needed for this purpose, arc lights were used in aerial search lights and certain film projectors.

Because of the noise they made, arc lamps were never very popular for home lighting. This didn't stop Latimer from attempting to improve them, however. A few wooden arc-lamp holders that he made can still be seen today. (These were included in a collection of early electrical devices put together by William T. Hammer. He apparently recognized that these devices would some day have great historical value. The Hammer collection has been displayed in several cities: at the Smithsonian Institution in Washington, D.C.; the Edison National Historic Site in West Orange, New Jersey; and Greenfield Village/Henry Ford Museum in Dearborn, Michigan.)

The years 1881 and 1882 were extremely busy ones for Lewis Latimer. His knowledge of electric lighting had become well known in the industry. He was therefore very much in demand. In addition to the patents and improvements he contributed to the electrical industry, Latimer also helped to install and operate some of the first electric plants in three major North American cities: New York City, Philadelphia, and Montreal. Under his direction, lighting was installed in railroad stations, large buildings, and on the streets of these big cities. His responsibilities included being in charge of producing the carbon filaments for the electric plants and supervising a large staff. In New York City, he lit the Equitable Building, the Union Club, Fisk and Hatch, and a number of other important buildings. In Philadelphia, Latimer and Maxim installed electric lighting in the offices of the *Philadelphia Ledger* newspaper.

After completing his work in Philadelphia, Latimer was sent to Montreal, Canada. His assignment there was "to fit up the railroad station and yards of Hochelagad with incandescent and arc lighting." But Latimer was presented with a new challenge in this city. His assistants and workmen spoke only French, so he had to learn the language well enough to write out their instructions. Because the work was so technical, Latimer's instructions had to be very precise. He had to write them in such a way that there would be no room for errors or misunderstanding. This was no easy task, and Latimer's achievement earned him great respect. In his journal, Latimer wrote: "This was my nightly lesson. My day was spent climbing telegraph poles and locating arc lamps on them with the assistance of my laborers who seemed much impressed with my effort to speak their native language."

After completing his work in Canada, Latimer returned to New York for a while. But he was soon sent to London, England, "to establish a factory there." Since Latimer was the only man in his company who understood every part of manufacturing these lamps, he was the best man for the job.

order we began to extend our
business and I went with Mr.
Maxim to Philadelphia to assist
him in putting in a plant in
the Philadelphia Ledger office, after
fitting up this plant I was dis-
patched to Montreal Canada to
fit up the railroad station
and yards of Hochelaga &
with incandescent and arc
lamps. As all of our assistants
were french speaking natives
I had to write out a list of
such orders as I must use
to make clear to my work men
what I wanted them to do, and
these orders I had to have the
clerk teach me to express in
french. This was my nightly
lesson, my day was spent
climbing telegraph poles and
locating arc lamps on them
with the assistance of my
laborers who earned much

*Latimer kept a journal, which includes a description of his work in
Montreal, Canada, in 1881.*

In the spring of 1882, therefore, Lewis and Mary Latimer were among the passengers of the *Ancoria* as it set sail for England. In her journal, Mary Latimer wrote about the time she spent in London. She described a leisurely life of letter writing, studying German, going for walks, shopping, and crocheting. She mentioned plans for an excursion to Paris and wrote about the drawings her husband did during their evenings at home. She found the London weather quite unusual and wrote,

> This is the strangest country I was ever in, about noontime the sun came out and as this was Ann's sweeping day thought I would go for walk while she was doing up the work…looked out the window and saw the fog just rolling over from the Nwest [Northwest] and in a few minutes there was a heavy or dense fog in less than half an hour could distinguish nothing in the street at all.

The weather wasn't the only thing that made the Latimers' life in London difficult. At the company, Lewis Latimer found a new challenge. Having coped with the language barrier in Montreal, Canada, he was now faced with a new dilemma. While Latimer did not need to learn a new language in London, he faced a different kind of challenge there. This time the barrier was the social-class distinctions of the company's British executives. They had a very difficult time accepting an American as the electrical expert. In his journal, Latimer observed: "The prevailing motif [general pattern of doing things] seemed to be humility of the workmen and the attitude that nothing that I can do can repay you for permitting me to earn an honest living."

Latimer and his assistant could not fake this feeling of humility that he refers to here. The English bosses reacted by trying to discredit them. Perhaps for the first time in his travels, Latimer was unhappy. He wrote: "They would write to the U.S. saying that we did not understand our business. The people in the U.S. having tested us in many cases simply wrote to us repeating the charge and we would see the leading men and explain and demonstrate the process to them so obscure."

Although Latimer's stay in London was not altogether pleasant, he succeeded in doing the job he had gone there to do—setting up the first lamp factory for Maxim's British Maxim—Weston Electric Light Company. He supervised the production of carbon filaments using the process he had invented. He also taught all the processes for production of the lamp—including glassblowing. Of the work he did in London, Latimer wrote:

> In nine months time we had the factory in running order with evay [Latimer's spelling] man familliar [his spelling again] with the particular branch of the man-afacture [his spelling] which fell to him, and as our easy independence was setting a bad example to the other work men, we were released from our contract and permitted to return to the U.S.

According to one source, Latimer accomplished his work in England three months ahead of schedule. Perhaps it is because he returned to the United States sooner than was expected that he found "the ranks [jobs] closed up and every place filled." In any event, it was at this point that Latimer stopped working for Hiram Maxim at the U.S. Electric Lighting Company. Perhaps he had become disenchanted with Maxim at last. Latimer's inventions had played an important role in the company's successful operations. Maxim had made huge profits from these inventions. Latimer may have come to feel that his efforts weren't appreciated. Around this time, Maxim wrote an autobiography in which he did not even mention Latimer. Perhaps this convinced Latimer that he was not truly valued by his longtime employer. (Although Maxim made no reference to Latimer, he did include a derogatory reference to African Americans.)

No one knows exactly what prompted Latimer to leave the company. It is possible that Maxim had temporarily turned his attention away from electric lighting and was now preoccupied with his new invention—the machine gun. This is the invention for which he is best known, even though he had been in the lighting industry from its early days. Maxim had also dabbled in other inventive enterprises. These included steam-powered airplanes and the self-regulating electrical generator. Whatever new glories Hiram Maxim went on to claim at this time, they did not include Lewis Latimer. Latimer was at the height of his career. The past two years—1881 and 1882—had been his most triumphant. He had received three patents—one of which was of far-reaching importance—and played a key role in lighting four of the world's great cities. In spite of these accomplishments, Latimer now found himself without a job.

CHAPTER

5

Electrical Expert for Edison

When Lewis Latimer left Hiram Maxim's company in 1883, his future did indeed look bleak. Opportunities did come along, however. But it was obvious that within a year Latimer's fortunes had made a 180 degree turn. Maxim's U.S. Electric Lighting Company was a leader in the industry both in the United States and abroad. Latimer had been a key figure in the company's success. But he now found himself having to accept positions at smaller, less stable companies. Latimer's fortunes were also affected by another development that made matters worse. From 1882 through 1885, the United States experienced an economic depression. Many people lost their jobs, and many companies went out of business.

According to Latimer's personal journal, he joined the Olmstead Electric Lighting Company in Brooklyn, New York, after leaving Maxim. He was draftsman and superintendent of lamp construction there. Olmstead, however, soon went out of business. Latimer then took a similar position with the Acme Electric Company in New York City. It was there that he began to manufacture the Latimer Lamp that can still be seen in the (William) Hammer Historical Collection. Unfortunately, Acme also went out of business. Following this, Latimer became draftsman and general assistant to Charles C. Perkins of the Imperial Electric Light Company. He went with Perkins to Hartford, Connecticut, to work with the Mather Electric Company.

On June 12, 1883—after ten years of marriage—Lewis and Mary Latimer became the proud parents of a baby daughter, Emma Jeanette Latimer. This was a happy time for the Latimers, but it must have been a very frustrating period for Lewis Latimer as well. Like most people with family responsibilities, he worried about the uncertainty of work. For a man who had so much to offer, this was especially trying.

Latimer's expertise had not gone unnoticed. Other giants in the electrical industry—such as Thomas Alva Edison—were very aware of his abilities and accomplishments. Edison's genius for assembling and tapping the talents of creative people was second only to his genius as an inventor. Latimer's affairs had reached their bleakest. Things seemed to be falling apart around him. It was during this period that Edison invited him to join the Edison Electric Light Company. The year was 1884. Latimer accepted the invitation. So began his long association with Edison.

More than anyone else in the electrical industry, Latimer had the qualifications that Edison needed at the moment. Latimer had been in the industry since it started, and he was one of the greatest experts in the business. His inventions had helped the industry to grow and prosper. In addition, he had worked for one of Edison's fiercest competitors—Hiram S. Maxim.

When Latimer first began to work at the Edison Electric Light Company, he was special assistant to Chief Counsel Richard N. Dyer. He worked out of the office at 65 Fifth Avenue in New York City, but he traveled a great deal. At this time, many inventors were patenting ideas that were related to the new electrical industry. As a result, many lawsuits were being filed by inventors as they tried to prove who had originated, or first thought up, an idea. Latimer's first job was to go to locations across the United States and gather information for use in lawsuits that involved Edison patents. When other inventors tried to use Edison's ideas without his permission, he would sue them to protect his inventions. Of course, other inventors brought lawsuits against Edison for the same reason.

As might be expected, Edison's greatest rival was Maxim. Maxim claimed to have patented the incandescent light bulb before Edison did. Many other inventors also contested, or questioned, Edison's claims. But these two giants in the industry were locked in what seemed to be one legal battle after another. Maxim and the others were able to continue in the electric light business while they waited for the outcome of the various lawsuits.

In 1886, a judge in St. Louis ruled in Maxim's favor. Edison was displeased and appealed the ruling. That meant the case would go to a higher court for another hearing. When Edison hired Latimer, he knew that Latimer would be of great value to him. He was right. Latimer knew every aspect of the electrical industry. Just as important in Edison's eyes, Latimer had worked for Maxim and was familiar with his operations. Latimer became an expert witness for Edison. An expert witness is a person called upon to provide special or technical knowledge at a trial or legal proceeding. Latimer's testimony frequently made the difference between

Thomas Alva Edison greatly benefited from Lewis Howard Latimer's knowledge, skill, and experience when he hired Latimer in 1884.

victory and defeat for Edison. Huge amounts of money could be gained or lost as the result of the verdict, or decision, handed down in a court case. Often millions of dollars were at stake. There was no denying Latimer's value to Edison and his light company

Latimer's contribution to the Edison Electric Light Company did not end with the victories he won for Edison in court. His next assignment was as a draftsman in the engineering department. Here he worked under John H. Vail. In 1890, Edison's legal department was formed under the direction of William J. Jenks. Latimer was immediately transferred to this department. He was then named the company's chief draftsman and patent expert. He continued to do much of the work he had been doing and was given new responsibilities as well. He made drawings for court exhibits and was in charge of the company's library. He inspected electrical plants that were believed to have infringed on Edison's patent rights. He also continued to testify in court. As Edison's patent expert, Latimer helped to prepare cases against Maxim and other inventors who challenged Edison's claims. He also did patent searches. He was able to put his knowledge of French and German to good use when he studied European patents. He often translated scientific articles into English for general use and court use.

While his career rose to great heights, other significant things took place in Latimer's life. On April 19, 1890, Mary Latimer gave birth to a new baby daughter, Louise Rebecca. She was named after her father, Lewis, and her grandmother, Rebecca Latimer. Now that his workdays were filled with the satisfaction that comes with hard work and achievements, Latimer could look forward to relaxed evenings with his family. He found great joy and happiness in the home he and his wife had made. Home was like a safe haven. There he was free from the competitiveness of the constant court cases. There he could enjoy a tranquil life with his wife and daughters.

Since childhood, Latimer had had a strong interest in writing and art. These interests had survived all the ups and downs of his life. They were his hobbies, and they had always been a very satisfying way to spend his leisure time. As a loving husband and father, he now enjoyed using his talents in writing and art to pay tribute to his family. For example, he wrote romantic love poems to his wife, Mary, and painted a portrait of their new baby.

Latimer's talents weren't limited to celebrating the joys of family life, however. During the same year in which his daughter Louise was born, Lewis Latimer used his gifts as an artist and writer to do something that he had never done before.

6

The Man Who Wrote the Book on Lighting

Lewis Howard Latimer wrote *the* book on lighting. He combined his skills as a writer and a draftsman with his thorough knowledge of the field of electricity. No one else had ever written a book that covered this subject so completely.

Latimer's book, *Incandescent Electric Lighting: A Practical Description of the Edison System*, was 140 pages long and was illustrated with his drawings. It was published by D. Van Nostrand & Company in 1890. The book was so highly regarded that it became "the bible"—the essential guidebook—for electrical engineers everywhere.

Here, in Latimer's own words, is an explanation of the way incandescent light is produced:

> If the electric current can be forced through a substance that is a poor conductor, it will create a degree of heat in that substance, which will be greater or less according to the quality of electricity forced through it. Upon this

principle of the heating effect of the electrical current, is based the operation of the incandescent lamp just described. Where copper and platinum wires readily conduct [carry] the current, the carbon filament offers a great deal of resistance to its passage, and for this reason becomes very hot, in fact is raised to white heat or incandescence, which gives its name to the lamp. You doubtless wonder why this thread of charcoal is not immediately consumed when in this state, but this is really accounted for when you remember, that without oxygen of the air, there can be no combustion [burning up of fuel] and that every possible trace of air has been removed from the bulb and is so thoroughly sealed up as to prevent admission of the air about it; and yet the lamp does not last forever, for the reason that the action of the current upon the carbon has a tendency to divide up its particles and transfer them from one point to another so that, sooner or later, the filament gives way at some point. Yet most of these lamps are guaranteed to last a thousand hours, and this at from four to six hours a day gives the lamp a life of several months.

Latimer's book was written as a tribute to Thomas Edison. It dealt only with the Edison system and must have made the inventor even more of a star than he already was. Edison must have been pleased. Apart from this, though, Latimer's book was a welcome source of information. The field of electric lighting was so new and there was so much interest in lighting cities and homes that such a book was very important. Although the book dealt with a subject that was not easy to understand, Latimer's ability to explain things clearly and briefly resulted in a slender volume. In fact, he received a letter from his publisher asking him to make the book longer. His solution was to ask two col-

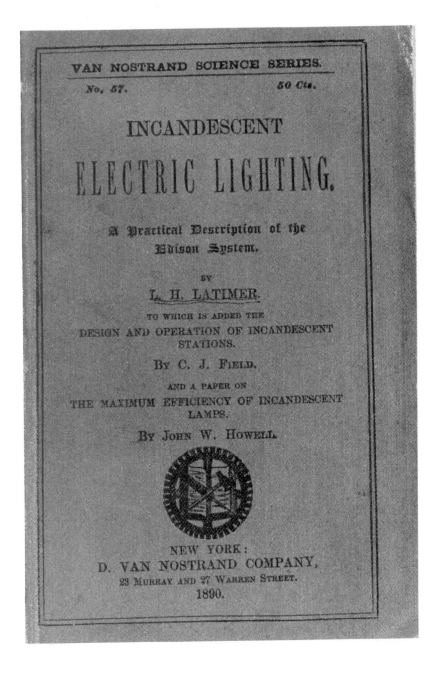

VAN NOSTRAND SCIENCE SERIES.

No. 57.   50 Cts.

INCANDESCENT
ELECTRIC LIGHTING.

A Practical Description of the
Edison System,

BY

L. H. LATIMER.

TO WHICH IS ADDED THE

DESIGN AND OPERATION OF INCANDESCENT
STATIONS.

BY C. J. FIELD,

AND A PAPER ON

THE MAXIMUM EFFICIENCY OF INCANDESCENT
LAMPS.

BY JOHN W. HOWELL.

NEW YORK:
D. VAN NOSTRAND COMPANY,
23 MURRAY AND 27 WARREN STREET.
1890.

leagues—Charles J. Fields and John W. Howell—to contribute details on the areas in which they specialized.

Legal battles are often fought for many years before the people involved receive a decision by the court. It was 1891 before the United States Circuit Court of Appeals of the Southern District of New York confirmed Edison's patents for incandescent light bulbs. As Edison had done before, Maxim, too, now appealed this ruling. Eventually, however, the court ruled in Edison's favor. There is no doubt that Latimer's knowledge of the electrical industry in general, and of Maxim's operations in particular, helped Edison to win this victory.

With Latimer's help, Edison won most but not all of his court battles. He was defeated twice by an inventor named Granville T. Woods. Sometimes referred to as the "Black Edison," Woods was an African American who was granted more than sixty patents for his inventions. Most of them were vital to the development of electrical and mechanical equipment. Many of his patents were credited to such companies as Westinghouse, American Bell Telephone, and General Electric. Woods's best-known invention is probably railroad telegraphy. His system made it possible for messages to be sent between moving trains and therefore made train travel much safer than it had been. Woods also designed the electromagnetic railway brake and a device that was used in telephones during the early 1900s. In his court battle with Edison, Woods was able to prove that he, not Edison, was the first inventor of the induction railway telegraph. Although they were temporarily adversaries, or enemies, in court, these two men obviously had great respect for each other's ability. One source states that Edison paid Woods $10,000 a year to be his consultant, or adviser.

Edison's battles were not limited to the courtroom.

Throughout the 1880s, Edison and Westinghouse Company (which bought Maxim's U.S. Electric Company) were engaged in "the battle of the currents." The debate was over the use of direct current versus alternating current. Both kinds of current come from a power source and travel through wires to homes or businesses. Once there the electricity provides energy needed for lights and machines that run by electricity. Alternating current changes direction at regular intervals. Its power source is called an alternator. Direct current goes in one direction. Its power source is a battery or generator.

Edison was convinced that direct current was better than alternating current. Westinghouse used only alternating current. Most electricians—including Latimer and others on Edison's staff—agreed that alternating current was the best choice. They were convinced that it was the most efficient way to distribute electricity to customers. But Edison insisted that it was dangerous. He felt so strongly about the issue that he was in favor of the use of the electric chair since it was powered by alternating current. He hoped that the public would be upset by this use of alternating current to take lives. He believed this would convince everyone that alternating current was truly dangerous. Because they knew that alternating current would eventually be accepted, members of Edison's staff tried to spare him the embarrassment of being proved wrong.

Edison had been involved in one type of dispute or another for many years. In 1892, he finally won the last of his many court battles with Maxim over patent claims. When the "patent wars" ended, the Edison and Westinghouse-Maxim people held secret meetings to discuss a possible merger of the two companies. That plan didn't work out, however. If it had, the new company could have changed to

Lewis Howard Latimer (second from the right), with the staff of the Legal Department, General Electric Company, 1894.

alternating current without embarrassing Edison. But something else happened in 1892. The Edison Electric Company became today's General Electric Company. The company was reorganized as a result of several mergers that took place. The decision regarding alternating current was no longer in Edison's hands.

7

Latimer's Creativity Continues

During all the years he spent with the Edison Electric Light Company and during his later work with patents, Latimer had used his know-how to defend many inventions by people other than himself. Yet he had been working on several inventions of his own. He simply did not have the time or the resources to develop many of his ideas. All the same, he didn't allow his creative talents to go to waste. Over the years, he had invented and patented a number of items. Some of these were electrical, and some were not.

A safety elevator and electrical fireworks were two of the inventions for which Latimer used his knowledge of electricity. Elevators had already been invented and were in use. They weren't as safe as Latimer believed they could and should be. He therefore found a way to make them safer. He described the merit of his improvement by stating "with it, an absolute fall of the elevator, is impossible." There are records of Latimer's lawyer writing to advise him on how he should go about submitting the invention to the Westinghouse and the Otis elevator companies. Apart from this, however, there seems to be no further correspondence about this invention. As for the electrical fireworks, a knowledgeable person at that time said that Latimer's patent had "points which will be of value in the future of electrical fireworks."

The field of electricity held great money-making possibilities because it was so new. It was also a field that Latimer knew from the inside out. For this reason, it would have been easy for him to ignore non-electrical solutions to many of the problems he saw around him. Instead, he was quick to use whatever solutions seemed most workable. In the spirit of a true inventor, Latimer always tried to find ways of making everyday life a little easier and more efficient.

Because experience had taught him that the best way to protect his ideas was to patent them, Latimer applied for and received several patents. U.S. Patent Number 557,076 was for *Locking Racks for Hats, Coats, and Umbrellas*. It was designed for use in such public places as restaurants and hotels. The racks held and locked articles securely. Latimer described this item as a "simple, efficient, and inexpensive device which will occupy very little space and which can be readily secured in position." It gave hotel and restaurant operators a solution to the problem of people getting their belongings mixed up. Many modern department stores still use a similar device today. Latimer applied for this patent in August 1895. It was issued on March 24, 1896. It had no model.

U.S. Patent Number 781,890 was for *A Book Supporter*. Latimer invented it to keep books from tipping over when they are arranged on a shelf side by side. The device not only kept books neatly arranged, but it also prevented them from becoming bent out of shape. Latimer described it this way:

If a given set of books fills a certain shelf, it is difficult to withdraw any selected book, while if the books do not exactly fill the shielf [shelf] some or all of the books tend to tip over more or less at the top, thereby causing one or more of the books to become distorted in shape by reason of the fact that the weight of books in their inclined position bears upon one edge of the cover or binding.

Other inventors had designed book supports, but Latimer's device was in some ways unique. As Latimer himself pointed out, it could be used as "a support either for the tops or bottoms of books arranged upon a shelf." Another advantage was that it could be "cut and pressed from a single piece of sheet metal, so that it has the advantage of being easily constructed and involving small expense." The book support was attached to the shelf at one end. It had a rest for books at the other. It was especially useful in libraries, where a large number of books were shelved. Latimer had such a great love of books that he may have designed the book supporter to help him care for his own large collection.

U.S. Patent Number 334,078 was an *Apparatus for Cooling and Disinfecting*. It was designed to make apartments, sickrooms, hospitals, and entire communities cooler, cleaner, and more sanitary. This invention served two functions. It had a large evaporation surface for cooling the air that passed over it and for charging the air with certain chemicals that destroyed harmful odors or germs. The device consisted of a frame over which a large piece of cloth had been stretched. At the bottom was a kind of trough that included the chemicals for disinfecting the room or area. Latimer even tried to design the invention so that it would fit in with the decoration of the location in which it would be used. In

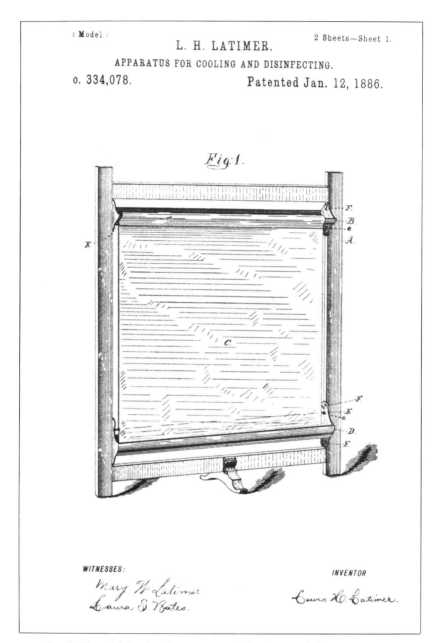

Lewis Howard Latimer's patent specifications and drawing for the model of his cooling and disinfecting apparatus, 1886.

UNITED STATES PATENT OFFICE.

LEWIS H. LATIMER, OF NEW YORK, N. Y.

APPARATUS FOR COOLING AND DISINFECTING.

SPECIFICATION forming part of Letters Patent No. 334,078, dated January 12, 1886.

Application filed September 3, 1885. Serial No. 176,058. (No model.)

To all whom it may concern:

Be it known that I, LEWIS H. LATIMER, a citizen of the United States, and a resident of New York, county of New York, and State of
5 New York, have invented certain new and useful Improvements in Devices for Cooling, Deodorizing, or Disinfecting Apartments, &c., of which the following is a specification.

The object of my invention is to present a
10 large evaporating-surface for the purpose of cooling the air about or passing over it, or to charge the same with chemical agents—such as carbolic acid, bromochloralum, &c.—to destroy such odors or germs of disease as may
15 exist therein, and I accomplish this object by stretching a webbing of any suitable textile fabric between a reservoir and drip-pan or between two or more reservoirs so arranged as to keep said webbing saturated and supply
20 the waste by evaporation.

My invention may be arranged in a variety of forms to adapt it to the place and purpose for which it is to be used; but whether used in a horizontal or vertical position for deodoriz-
25 ing, disinfecting, or cooling, the device only varies in the means adopted for holding it in place, the main features—to wit, the reservoirs and webbing—always remaining the same or only slightly modified in shape.

30 In the accompanying drawings, forming part of this specification, Figure 1 is a perspective view of a screen embodying my invention. Fig. 2 is a perspective view of the upper reservoir; Fig. 3, a vertical cross-section of the
35 same; Fig. 4, a like section of the lower reservoir, and Fig. 5 a modification thereof.

The screen-frame A (see Fig. 1) has mounted in its upper end a trough or reservoir, B, secured to the frame by screws F passing through
40 openings f in the ends of the reservoir, this reservoir having at either end, below the trough, a socket, e, to receive the ends of a rod, E, which passes through the upper portion of a webbing, C, at a suitable distance from the
45 edge thereof, so as to leave a flap sufficiently long to pass up to and lie in the trough B. The lower end of the webbing C has also a rod, E, passing through it, which is held in sockets e at either end of the reservoir D, and
50 just above the trough thereof, the webbing continuing below the rod down into the trough of the reservoir.

Instead of the rods E the reservoir B may be provided with a tube, G, passing below
55 and parallel with the axis thereof and supplied with a valve, H, by which the passage of the liquid from the reservoir may be regulated, Fig. 5. The tube G, provided with openings g g g on its upper side, passes through a hem
60 in the upper end of the webbing, the liquid admitted from the reservoir through the opening g' overflowing through the openings g g g and keeping the webbing saturated.

Where the device is to be used as a curtain
65 or awning, the reservoirs are supported by brackets instead of being held in a frame. The liquid is drawn off through the tube b, Fig. 3.

Where it is desired to cool an apartment, the device, in the form of a curtain, is secured to
70 the window-frames by brackets attached to the upper and lower reservoirs, and is held parallel to the window and about a foot away therefrom. The webbing is then saturated with water and stretched between the reservoirs
75 with its opposite ends dipping therein, one or both of the reservoirs being also supplied with water to be drawn into the webbing by capillary attraction. The warm air entering the apartment by the windows comes in contact
80 with the moist surface of the webbing, evaporating the water therefrom, parting with some of its heat in doing so, and creating a motion in the air of the room resulting in both cooling and changing the latter.

85 In neighborhoods where unpleasant odors or malarious exhalations exist deodorizing or disinfecting liquids may be substituted for the water or added thereto.

In sick-rooms or hospitals, where disinfect-
90 ing or deodorizing are the sole objects sought, the device may be used in the form of a screen, as shown in Fig. 1.

I am aware that textile fabrics of various kinds have heretofore been used in connection
95 with chemicals for deodorizing and cooling purposes. I therefore do not claim, broadly, this principle of disinfecting or cooling the atmosphere of an apartment.

Having described my invention, what I
100 claim as new, and desire to secure by Letters Patent, is—

In a deodorizing and cooling device for apartments, the combination consisting of a frame, the trough or reservoir mounted on said frame

describing the invention for the patent application, Latimer said, "It can be formed into any configuration [shape or style]." He went on to say that the apparatus could even be used as a curtain.

Latimer's wife, Mary W. Latimer, was a witness for the disinfecting apparatus. (Inventors, before they file their official patent application with the government, take certain steps to prove that they thought up the ideas for the invention. They usually draw a sketch of the invention, and they write a description of it. Then they have two witnesses watch as they sign and date these documents.) Mary Latimer took a keen interest in the things that interested her husband. It was obvious that he, in turn, tried to include his family in his work whenever he could. As the Latimer girls grew up, they, too, took an active interest in the things that interested their father. Latimer liked playing his violin or flute for relaxation, and the girls shared their father's enjoyment of music. Sometimes they even created their own sheet music. Jeanette composed the words and the music, and Louise illustrated it. They then sold copies of their compositions. Their father, of course, bought more copies than anyone else.

In his leisure time, Latimer liked to make drawings of the people he had observed. Two pictures that reflect his travels are of a Greek beggar and an Italian child. Latimer also used artistic abilities to design his own bookplates. Bookplates are identifying labels that can be pasted into a book to show who owns it. They were elaborately decorated and more popular in Latimer's day than they now are.

It was obvious that the Latimer girls had inherited their father's creative talent. Jeanette was drawn to a career in music. Louise's interest was in art. Unlike his own parents,

A color portrait of an Italian boy, signed by Latimer in 1894.

Lewis Latimer could afford to educate his children. Both girls were sent to fine specialized schools where they could develop their talents. Living in New York City was a great advantage. Many of the finest specialized schools were located there.

Emma Jeanette, who preferred her middle name, Jeanette, to her first name, studied at the Juilliard School of Music. She became an accomplished musician. The composer Harry T. Burleigh wrote a song entitled "Jean" in her honor. She had a promising career as a concert pianist before marrying Gerald Norman, a noted teacher in New York. The program of her Philadelphia concert is preserved in the Latimer Papers at the New York Public Library's Schomburg Center for Research in Black Culture. Jeanette decided to devote her time and talents to her two children, Winifred and Gerald. Not surprisingly, she taught her children music. Both children's middle names were Latimer. They brought their grandfather great pleasure. They grew up with fond recollections of good times spent with him at the family home in Flushing, Queens, New York.

The Latimers' younger daughter, Louise, wanted to be called "Reba." She studied at the Pratt Institute, where she developed her artistic abilities. She became a public-school teacher and was able to enrich the lives of her students.

It is not surprising that Lewis Latimer's daughters chose careers in music and art. Throughout their childhood, they had seen their father take pleasure in the arts. He was their role model, and he was always there. What is, perhaps, surprising is that Lewis Latimer's own interests may have been shaped by those of his father—George Latimer. Lewis Latimer was a young boy when his father left the family. He did not have the good fortune to have his own father as an ever-present role model. Yet both he and his father were writers!

Lewis's father, George Latimer, wrote poetry and possibly completed an autobiography. Winifred Latimer Norman has a copy of a poem written by her great-grandfather, George Latimer. The poem is titled "Songs for Freedom." Its theme is freedom from bondage and is religious in nature.

When George Latimer was seventy-three years old, he was interviewed by John Wallace Hutchinson of the family who had sung at protest meetings, during the time that Latimer was being held in jail. Hutchinson was in the process of writing a book, and George Latimer said that he, too, was writing his reminiscences. It is possible that he completed them. Hutchinson published the interview with George Latimer in the appendix of his book.

That interview and an interview Latimer had given to the editors of the *Latimer Journal* back in 1842 give many details of his life. Some historians believe that George went to England and anonymously wrote a book based on his life. That book was entitled *The White Slave*. There was a good reason why Latimer might have written anonymously. If specific details such as names and places were given in slave narratives, the authors placed themselves in danger of being recaptured. This actually happened to Frederick Douglass. Like George Latimer, Douglass had started life as a slave in the South, made a daring escape, and for years lived in danger of being taken back into slavery. In fact, Douglass was still in danger at the time he worked for George Latimer's freedom. But unlike Latimer, Douglass was not located by his slave owner—that is, until he wrote his life story. Since

Latimer knew Frederick Douglass, he realized how risky it was to write specific details. He had avoided re-enslavement once and did not want to take that chance again.

No one will ever know for sure whether—or how— George Latimer's interest in writing was passed on to his son Lewis. Was it heredity? Did Lewis have childhood memories that made him associate his father with writing? Or was it just a coincidence that father and son shared this interest?

Although Lewis spent only the first ten years of his life with his father, those early years were very important. During those years, Lewis spent afternoons and evenings working with his father. It is entirely possible that as the two worked in the barbershop or hung wallpaper together, they talked about writing. After all, this was one of Lewis's favorite school subjects. Since it was an interest his father shared, they probably discussed it. Since he had been separated from his father at an early age, Lewis would certainly have cherished the memory of happy times they spent together.

8

Lessons in Loyalty

Many of the things that have been written about Lewis Latimer fail to indicate that he was eventually reunited with his father. The most definite evidence of this can be found in a letter that Lewis Latimer received in 1894. The letter was from none other then Frederick Douglass, the former slave who had become a statesman, an orator, and a newspaper editor since the days when he worked with other abolitionists to gain George Latimer's freedom.

It is obvious from Douglass's letter sent in answer to a letter that Lewis Latimer had written to him. Douglass's letter began:

I give you thanks for your excellent letter. It made me proud of you. I was glad to hear of your mother and family. I saw your father for [a] Moment in Boston last

A copy of Frederick Douglass's 1894 letter to Lewis Howard Latimer.

Spring. He seemed in good health then and I am surprised to learn of his condition now. It is fifty two years since I first saw your father and mother in Boston. You can hardly imagine the excitement the attempts to recapture them caused in Boston....

George Latimer had been living near Boston—in Lynn, Massachusetts—during most of the years between the time he left his family and the time of Douglass's letter. Lynn was the same city from which Frederick Douglass had written William Lloyd Garrison many years earlier when he sought support for George Latimer's freedom. In November 1894, a then-elderly George Latimer was interviewed by John W. Hutchinson. Latimer, seventy-three, was described as a man "with a handsome pair of gray side whiskers as those of any prosperous retired banker." He was carrying a cane, for he was paralyzed on one side. In that interview, George Latimer stated that for "forty-five years I pursued the trade of a paperhanger in Lynn."

Frederick Douglass's letter proved that George Latimer was appearing in public in 1894. Douglass and Latimer probably saw each other at the People's Church in Boston. Douglass gave a lecture there on May 10. John W. Hutchinson wrote that he and George Latimer had attended the lecture together and he introduced Latimer at the end of the program.

It is significant that Lewis Latimer had mentioned his parents and his father's health problems in a letter to Douglass. This suggests that Lewis Latimer had his parents' well-being at heart. Lewis Latimer's journal reveals that he had unpleasant memories of the farm school that he had been sent to because of family circumstances. As he grew up, he probably realized how limited his parents' choices had been as runaway slaves. This insight may have softened any bitter feelings he had felt, but his journal for his later years does not record much in the way of personal feelings.

Lewis Latimer had spent most of his childhood and all of his adult life working. Apart from the periods of relaxation he enjoyed with his family, it might seem as if there was little time for anything else. But Latimer did have time for friends and activities that enriched his and others' lives in one way or another. One of his friends was Richard Theodore Greener. Greener may have been Latimer's friend since childhood. He was about Latimer's age and had also grown up in the Boston area. He was the first African American to graduate from Harvard University. Greener became a scholar, lawyer, librarian, and diplomat.

Latimer and Greener were very young men when the Civil War ended. Although they went into different types of work, they respected each other's intellect and had similar social concerns. For example, they both wanted to see former slaves and their families move smoothly from slavery to full citizenship.

There were many adjustments to be made all at once during the post–Civil War period known as Reconstruction. Families that had been separated as the result of slavery were trying to find lost relatives. Some newly freed men and women stayed where they'd lived during slavery and continued to work for their former masters at low wages. Many rented land or gave a large part of their crops to the landowners for the use of the land. Some were eventually able to save enough money to buy the land they lived on, although many former masters refused to sell land or overcharged for it. Many newly freed men and women had to relocate and start a new life in big cities. As slaves, they had not been paid for their labor, and they had no money with which to buy land. Many former slaves either lacked job skills that were needed in the cities, or they were discriminated against when they tried to find work.

Although in 1868 the Fourteenth Amendment to the U.S. Constitution guaranteed equal protection for everyone under the law, it was not always practiced. Most former slaves had been denied the chance to learn to read and write. Yet they wished to gain their full rights and responsibilities as American citizens. Getting an education and gaining the right to vote were considered the two most important ways to improve living and working conditions.

Latimer was well aware of the difficulties faced by newly freed slaves. Throughout his adult life he worked, often very quietly, to smooth the changes that had to be made on the way from enslavement to full citizenship. He had personally experienced the pain that resulted from the hardships his own parents had known.

It was through Richard Theodore Greener that Latimer became involved in national civil rights issues. Greener was especially interested in politics, and his letters to Latimer show that he really liked living in Washington, D.C. In 1873, Greener became the associate editor of the *New National Era*, which was published in that city. This was a newspaper that had been edited by Frederick Douglass and later by Douglass's son.

An outstanding intellectual, Greener was chairman of the Department of Metaphysics and Logic at the University of South Carolina during the mid-1870s. In 1875 he served as university librarian at the University of South Carolina. There he reorganized the library and prepared a catalog. While holding this position, Greener completed his law degree and was admitted to the bar, that is, was able to be a lawyer, in both South Carolina and the District of Columbia. He also served on a commission that set up free public schools for all children in South Carolina.

The period of Reconstruction came to an end in 1877. At the University of South Carolina, where Greener taught, African Americans were again being denied their right to an education. Greener left South Carolina and became an instructor and later the dean of the law department at Howard University in Washington, D.C. He was a man of many achievements. He went on to hold a number of positions in government. Greener was appointed secretary of the Grant Monument Association in New York State.

Greener also served as chief examiner of New York City's municipal civil service board, which tested people who wanted to work for the city.

Greener was fortunate enough to be able to support himself after he left the University of South Carolina at the end of Reconstruction. Many other African Americans in the South were not so fortunate. Their rights as American citizens were not being respected. Their land was being taken away. They were being threatened, injured, and sometimes even killed by lawless groups of white people. Their right to vote was no longer protected, although in 1870 the Fifteenth Amendment to the U.S. Constitution had guaranteed that it would be. Southern blacks searched for solutions to these problems. Many decided to go where they could start a new life.

Greener was in favor of migration of former slaves to the fertile lands of Kansas and other western states. Lands in these areas were being advertised at low prices. Greener served as national secretary of the Emigration Aid Society. In this position, he participated in a debate with Frederick Douglass at the American Social Science Association Congress. This gathering was held in Saratoga Springs, New York, in September 1879. Douglass opposed the "Great Exodus," as it was called, to Kansas. He believed that although African Americans faced many difficulties in the South, this was their home. They had survived the hardships of slavery. Even though they again faced many obstacles, they should stay put. They had worked too long and too hard to leave familiar surroundings and go to Kansas where they'd be total strangers. Like Latimer, both Greener and Douglass cared deeply about the plight of the newly freed men, women, and children. But they had different ideas about the solution to the problem.

The "Great Exodus" that Douglass and Greener had debated ended in disappointment. The 20,000 to 40,000 people who had left the southern states to go to Kansas found neither Kansas nor the South to be the "promised land" they hoped for. In 1895, Greener wanted Latimer to attend a meeting of the National Conference of Colored Men in Detroit, Michigan. Latimer was unable to attend the conference, but he wrote a spirited statement in which he expressed passionately and beautifully his sorrow at the wrongs being done to African Americans in the United States.

I am heart and soul in the movement, because

(1) it is necessary that we should show the people of this country that we who have by our martyrdom [suffering] under the lash; by our heroism on the battlefield; by our Christian forbearance [patience] beneath an overwhelming burden of injustice; and by our submission to the laws of the native land, proven ourselves worthy citizens of our common country.

(2) Because there is no separation of the colored Americans from those of the white American, and it is our duty to show our country, and ...the world that we are looking to the interests of the country at large, when we protest against the crime and injustice meted out [given] to any class or conditions of our citizens.

(3) Because the commumity which permits a crime against its humblest member to go unpunished is nursing into life and strength a power which will ultimately threaten its own existence.

(4) Because our history conclusively proves that the attempt to degrade [lower and take away the rights of] any portion, class, or race of our common people has

always been fraught with [has always carried with it] more danger to the oppressor than the oppressed.

(5) Because an evenhanded justice to all, under and through the law, is the only safe course to pursue for where might makes right, brute strength will supersede [overcome] intelligence in the control of our communities....

Latimer went on to say:

These are a few of the reasons why we should have a National Convention, and if that Convention, forgetting all other considerations directs its energies to presenting its cause before the people, as it affects the people at large, presenting it as our fathers did the question of slavery, with facts and figures, showing, as it can be shown, that where the Colored American is lynched [murdered by mob action], the white American is assassinated; that ignorance and crime go hand in hand with prejudice; that schools and churches multiply where there is neither class nor color distinctions in the law; that class legislation puts a premium [high value] on ignorance and illiteracy, in that it aids a man to think himself superior by accident of birth than by the achievements of merit and ability. If our cause be made the common cause, and all our claims and demands be founded on justice and humanity, recognizing that we must wrong no man in winning OUR rights, I have faith to believe that the Nation will respond to our plea for equality before the law, security under the law, and an opportunity, by and through maintenance of the law, to enjoy with our fellow citizens of all races and complexions the blessings guaranteed us under the Constitution, of "life, liberty, and the pursuit of happiness."

9

Time Brings Change

While Latimer and Greener were working for social changes, other changes greatly affected Lewis Latimer's life.

At the age of forty-six, Latimer signed a "Declaration for Invalid Pension." His reason for doing so was stated as follows, "Defective eyesight to such an extent as [to] debar him from performing any active manual labor." In spite of his poor eyesight, he managed for many years to remain productive, doing work that, more than most jobs, depended on excellent vision.

Following the reorganization of the Edison Company, there was talk of a merger with the Westinghouse Company. The merger plans were never carried out. In 1896, however, the two companies cooperated in establishing the Board of Patent Control. The many years of legal battles had left both companies almost bankrupt. They decided that the Board of Patent Control was in the best interests of both companies.

Its purpose was to prevent further patent lawsuits between these two companies or any other company.

William J. Jenks, who had been in charge of Edison's legal department, now headed the new board. Latimer was selected as chief draftsman and expert witness. Having seen him in action during their court battles, Edison and Westinghouse representatives were convinced that he was the best man for the job. He served in this position as long as the Board of Patent Control was in operation.

Lewis Latimer's father died in Lynn, Massachusetts, in May of the year that the Board of Patent Control was formed. That same year the U.S. Supreme Court handed down a decision that had far-reaching effects.

The important 1896 decision was the outcome of the *Plessy* v. *Ferguson* case. The Court ruled that it was constitutional to have "separate but equal" facilities for black and white citizens. In reality, the decision made racial segregation legal. This was the beginning of "Jim Crow" laws that legally enforced separation of whites and blacks on trains and streetcars, in restaurants, hotels, and restrooms, and in many other facilities. These separate facilities were seldom equal. Most often the facilities designated for blacks were inferior to those for whites.

Even so, people like Richard Theodore Greener continued to try to work for fairness through the political process. In 1897, he wrote Lewis Latimer a letter from Washington, D.C., that began, "My dear ole man." In the letter he told Latimer that there was a great scramble for government jobs there. He thought that if Latimer wanted a job, his scientific ability would be in demand. He also mentioned in the letter that Booker T. Washington, the president of Tuskegee Institute, was going to be in New York soon. That may be how Latimer first made contact with Booker T. Washington. Washington had set up the Tuskegee Institute to train African Americans in various technical trades. Washington favored instilling African Americans with the values of hard work and self-help and opposing demands for an end to the "separate but equal" doctrine. Latimer later received a letter from Washington in which he expressed his interest in having Latimer draw a layout, or plan, of the buildings and grounds of the Tuskegee campus.

During this time, Latimer corresponded with a number of other friends and business associates. Among his papers at the Schomburg Center for Research in Black Culture are many of these letters. There are letters about poems he had sold for publication, correspondence from the National Association of Negro Authors, and a thank-you note from a Willing Workers group for which Latimer had written and directed a comedy. Latimer sent some of his poetry to composer Rosamond Johnson. Rosamond Johnson was best known for writing with his brother, James Weldon Johnson, "Lift Every Voice and Sing," often referred to as the "Black National Anthem." Johnson wrote to Latimer to express interest in setting some of Latimer's poetry to music. Latimer sent a Fourth of July poem to Thomas Edison in the hope that Edison would read it as part of an Independence Day celebration to be recorded on a phonograph record—the phonograph being an Edison invention. Although there is no evidence of the poem's being recorded in this way, a letter shows that Edison did read the poem very carefully and thought it was very good.

Latimer did not limit his letter writing to pleasant exchanges with friends and business associates. When situations arose that Latimer felt compelled to respond to, he often did so by letter. In 1902, Latimer wrote such a letter to Mayor Seth Low of New York City. In this letter, he expressed his concern that Low had failed to reappoint S. R. Scottron to the Brooklyn School Board. This left the board without an African-American representative. Latimer then headed a petition drive to collect three hundred signatures of others who felt as he did. This, too, was sent to the mayor. Here is part of Latimer's letter:

> Since you represent ALL the people in this city, and since all races and nationalities forming part of this heterogeneous citizenship [group of citizens of many different backgrounds] have their due consideration from the appointmenting powers, we feel no hesitation in asking that our representative, Mr. S.R. Scottron, be considered. Not alone as our representative, but as a good citizen, a worthy gentleman, and one whose influence in his native city warrants the assertion [deserves the claim] that he would be a bit representative of any of her people, regardless of racial differences.

In his quiet way, Latimer had become an eloquent spokesman for the rights of African Americans. But his concern for people and his willingness to become involved in issues that affected them wasn't limited to African Americans. When in 1906, he was asked to help at the Henry Street Settlement, he gladly did so.

The settlement house had been founded in New York City in 1893 by Lillian Wald. This community organization provided job training, recreation, and health services to immigrants. Most of these immigrants were Eastern European Jews who arrived in the United States in the late 1800s and early 1900s. With his work on the Board of Patent

Control and his interests outside of work, Latimer had plenty to do. He could easily have said that he didn't have the time to take on any more responsibilities. But he didn't say that.

In many ways, the immigrants were like Latimer's father. Although they weren't being hunted by slave catchers, they were wretchedly poor, as George Latimer had been. Many had left terrible economic or social conditions in their homelands. Others had been persecuted or mistreated because of their religious beliefs. Finally, they had come to the United States in search of a better life and could not speak English. He saw similarities between the oppression the immigrants faced and the oppression his parents and ancestors had experienced as slaves. He had a strong commitment to the belief that everyone should be given opportunities to develop his or her potential.

Latimer soon began teaching English and mechanical drawing at the settlement house. (Mechanical drawing is technical drawing done with the help of instruments such as a compass. These drawings are needed to show how such things as machines, buildings, and inventions are built or used.) The information and skills he taught the immigrants in these courses were of great value to them as they tried to adjust to their new life in the United States.

Perhaps Latimer also took the time to teach classes at the Henry Street Settlement because he had grown up knowing the importance of stopping to help someone in need. During his childhood, he had heard his parents talk about how such busy men as William Lloyd Garrison and Frederick Douglass had worked to help his father gain freedom from slavery. He knew how hard these abolitionists had worked to publicize and raise money for George Latimer's fugitive-slave case.

In Tribute To

Lewis H. Latimer
(1848–1928)

Inventor   Author
Poet Musician Teacher
Humanist

The self-educated son of a run-away slave, whose brilliant achievements and creative spirit led to the development of the light bulb, the telephone, and the Age of Electricity.

A man of international fame and honor, who shared his talents with the Henry Street Settlement.

In recognition of the time and knowledge he so generously gave us.

Presented to Ms. Winifred Latimer Norman on this date of February 5, 1976 by the Henry Street Settlement.

Bertram M. Beck
Bertram M. Beck
Executive Director

Atkins Preston
Atkins Preston
Associate Executive Dir.

Winifred Latimer Norman received this tribute to her grandfather from the Henry Street Settlement.

84

It was while working on George Latimer's behalf that Frederick Douglass made his first attempts at writing. He had only recently become active in the abolitionist movement. Although both George Latimer and Frederick Douglass had been skilled craftsmen when they gained their freedom, both had difficulty earning enough money to support their families. Of the two men, only Douglass had an opportunity to develop his full potential. In addition to becoming an author and editor, Douglass at one time or another had been a ship caulker, an abolitionist, an orator, a reformer, a conductor on the Underground Railroad, an adviser to President Abraham Lincoln, the president of the Freedman's Bank, a fighter for women's rights, marshal of the District of Columbia, and the U.S. consul-general to the Republic of Haiti.

By the time Lewis Latimer began to work at the Henry Street Settlement, all the events surrounding Frederick Douglass's and George Latimer's early lives were in the distant past. Former slaves no longer lived in fear of being found by slave catchers and forced back into slavery. The Civil War had long since ended, and slavery had been abolished for more than forty years. People like Latimer and Greener were now working hard to provide a place for everyone in the United States.

For more than twenty years before he began working at the Henry Street Settlement, Latimer had been active in helping former slaves and their descendants in their search for a better life. Even though he had gotten to develop many of his own talents, he was very much aware that many people were still struggling to overcome such disadvantages as poor education. He firmly believed this statement he wrote in one of his essays: "We create our future, by well improving present opportunities: however few and small they may be."

In his own life, Lewis Latimer had overcome many obstacles that would have discouraged someone with less determination. Although he held important positions in and made valuable contributions to the electrical industry, he never forgot his impoverished beginnings and the terrible toll poverty took on his family's life.

Recognition as a Pioneer

Lewis Latimer was a man to whom spiritual beliefs and lifelong loyalties were important. In these, as in other areas of his life, he thought and felt deeply—and took action.

In 1908, Lewis Latimer and other like-minded people founded the Flushing (New York) Unitarian Church. The church introduced its members to the teachings of many different world religions. Unitarianism placed emphasis on the importance of character and of tolerance of differing religious views. This must have appealed to Latimer.

Also, it is possible that Latimer's interest in the Unitarian Church began in childhood. The topic of religion may well have come up as he worked side by side with his father. George Latimer may have told his son, Lewis, about another father-and-son team. William Francis Channing was one of the editors of the *Latimer Journal*, the newspaper that had publicized George Latimer's case. This editor's father was the Reverend Dr. William Ellery Channing, the organizer of the American Unitarian Association. One of

Channing's sermons was considered to be the definitive statement of Unitarian beliefs. So Lewis Latimer may have had an interest in these beliefs many years before he helped found the Flushing Unitarian Church.

Latimer remained an active member of the church for as long as his health permitted. His role as a founder was acknowledged by the setting up of the Lewis Howard Latimer Award. The church's sixtieth anniversary booklet contains an excellent brief biography of Latimer. It describes how talented he was in many areas. His wife, children, and other relatives were also active in the church. His granddaughter, Winifred Latimer Norman, not only participated in the Unitarian (now Unitarian-Universalist) church at a local level. She also held positions at the church's national and international levels.

The Flushing Unitarian Church wasn't the only organization that Latimer regarded highly. For many years he belonged to and for a time was a staff officer of the George Huntsman Post of the Grand Army of the Republic (GAR). The GAR was an organization made up of Civil War veterans who had served in the Union army or navy. It worked to preserve the memory of Union soldiers and sailors who had died during the war. It also pressed the government to provide such benefits as pensions for veterans. Photographs taken at the time reveal the pride Latimer took in being a member of the GAR. Serving in the Civil War was an experience that meant a lot to Latimer. He continued to enjoy the comradeship of others who had fought to end slavery. He spent many pleasant hours at the post.

During working hours, Latimer's duties at the Board of Patent Control continued until the board was abolished in 1911. The electrical companies that had at first cooperated in its formation had later disagreed on its operation.

Latimer then became a patent consultant for Edwin W. Hammer, a New York City engineer and patent lawyer. Hammer had been chief technical assistant on the Board of Patent Control, so the two men had known each other personally and professionally for quite some time. In fact, Latimer had known and worked with both Edwin Hammer and Hammer's brother, William. The Hammer brothers had great respect for Latimer's work. William Hammer became a collector of Latimer's lamps and other early electrical devices. (This collection is a valuable resource to present-day researchers. If William Hammer had not made the effort to collect models of these electrical devices, they would probably have been thrown away.) A letter written in 1971 by Leah S. Burt of the Edison National Historical Site gives some idea of the number of lamps that were invented during the late nineteenth century:

> I would imagine that within the ten-year period from Edison's invention of the first successful incandescent lamp in October 1879, there might easily have been several thousand patents issued to different inventors. Edison himself took out about eighty patents on the lamp during those same ten years....
>
> Each patent is usually only a small advance in the whole art of lighting, as a patent is issued concerning each detail, such as the type of filament, the method of connecting it to the lead-in wires, the method of creating a vacuum, etc.

This letter gives some insight into why people living in the 1880s may not have paid close attention to every lamp that was invented. There was a great deal of interest in lighting improvements. But unless people were working within the lighting industry, they probably didn't keep up

Latimer drew this sketch showing himself as a consulting engineer for Hammer and headed for what he called an "uncertain future." He labeled the sketch, "My situation as it looked to me in 1912."

with every development that came along. It is because Hammer placed different models of Latimer's arc and incandescent lamps in his collection that they exist more than a hundred years after they were first manufactured. Some of them still work.

Perhaps the greatest honor Lewis Latimer received during his lifetime was that of becoming a charter—that is, one of the first—member of the Edison Pioneers. This organization was made up of the men who had created the electrical industry. Formed in 1918, the Edison Pioneers carried on the ideals and goals of Thomas Alva Edison. All twenty-eight charter members had worked with Edison before 1885. Being one of the original twenty-eight Edison Pioneers was the highest possible honor in the entire electrical industry. Lewis Howard Latimer and Edwin and William Hammer were members of this distinguished group of scientists.

Years of working together and being members of the Edison Pioneers had created a warm, lasting friendship between Lewis Latimer and Edwin Hammer. When Lewis and Mary Latimer celebrated their fiftieth wedding anniversary in 1923, Hammer wrote: "Our sincerest congratulations and best wishes accompany this note. A fiftieth Anniversary does not come to many married couples and only once to any, so you see how fortunate you are. It speaks well for both of you...." The letter went on to say that the "Pioneers all speak of him highly and affectionately, and each succeeding generation seems to have fallen into the same pleasant habit." It was signed by all the members of Hammer's staff and their spouses.

Latimer continued his professional association with Edwin Hammer—whose firm later became known as Hammer & Schwarz—until poor health forced him to retire in

The Edison Pioneers in 1918.

1924. During his long, distinguished career as an electrical engineer, Latimer had perfected the manufacture of carbon filaments, personally supervised the installation of lighting in major cities of the world, and made significant contributions to the success of both Thomas Edison and Hiram Maxim.

Lewis Latimer was a giant among giants in what was probably one of the most important technologies ever developed in the history of humankind.

11

Latimer's Legacy

When Lewis and Mary Latimer grew older, their daughter Louise lived in the family home at 137–53 Holly Avenue so that she could care for her parents. Jeanette and her family lived only a block away on Juniper Street. She and her husband and children were able to look in on her parents every day.

Mary Wilson Latimer died before her husband did. Her death occurred in 1924. She was buried in Oakwood Cemetery in her hometown of Fall River, Massachusetts. In addition to the pain and sorrow of losing his wife, Latimer had to deal with his own failing health. For almost half his life, he had had problems with his vision. During the years that he was making very detailed drawings, the most powerful light bulbs were only 36 candlepower, which was dim compared with today's lights. Yet he had managed to continue productive work for many years. As he aged, Latimer suffered from increasing problems with his eyesight. His health problems grew worse when he suffered a

*Lewis and Mary Latimer and one of their daughters on the porch of
their house in Flushing, Queens, New York.*

stroke and was paralyzed on one side—just as his father had been.

Latimer had spent his life making contributions to the electrical industry in which inventors as talented as Latimer had made fortunes. However, Latimer had not become a wealthy man. He received a pension of $17.50 a week from the Edison Company and a military pension of $72 a month.

After a life of overcoming one challenge after another, Lewis Latimer had begun to give up the fight. His daughters were saddened by this change in their father. Feeling that he needed something to spark his interest in living, they arranged to have a book of his poems printed in honor of his seventy-seventh birthday in 1925. Latimer's book of poetry was called *Poems of Life and Love*. A limited number of copies were privately printed for the occasion. They were beautiful. The little volume included lovely photographs of Latimer's beloved wife, Mary, and of their daughters, Jeanette and Louise. It was divided into a section of poems about life and a section about love. This is one of the "poems of life." It is simply called "Friends."

Friend of my childhood,
Of life's early days
When together we wandered
Through bright sunny ways
Each true to the other,
Till full manhood came,
And found the old friendship
As ever the same.

Came summer and winter,
Years waxed and waned.
Youth it had left us

But friendship remained
And now as with white locks
I bend o'er life's page,
The friend of my childhood
Is the friend of my age.

"Ebon Venus" is the best known of Latimer's "poems of love":

Let others boast of maidens fair,
Of eyes of blue and golden hair;
My heart like needles ever true
Turns to the maid of ebon hue.

I love her form of matchless grace.
The dark brown beauty of her face,
Her lips that speak of love's delight,
Her eyes that gleam as stars at night.

O'er marble Venus let them rage,
Who set the fashions of the age;
Each to his taste, but as for me,
My Venus shall be ebony.

Lewis Latimer died at his home at the age of eighty. He was buried near his wife. Lengthy obituaries—notices of his death—appeared in major newspapers across the United States.

Latimer's life spanned three very important periods in the history of the United States: slavery, Reconstruction, and the last quarter of the nineteenth century and the first quarter of the twentieth. All three periods were marked by social and technological changes that dramatically changed life in the United States and the world. Throughout it all,

Lewis Latimer moved quietly from one challenge to another. There were many ups and downs. There were times, too, when everything seemed to have come to a standstill. But Latimer always made an effort to learn and to prove his ability whenever he had an opportunity to do so. In the end, victory was his.

Still, it wasn't possible for Latimer to forget that he was the son of slaves. At the beginning of Latimer's career, for example, Hiram Maxim was "amazed" to find him working as a draftsman. This was because African Americans had constantly been denied opportunities to get training and to work in technical fields. Even after he learned to be a draftsman, Latimer might easily have spent his life doing odd jobs that led nowhere. During Latimer's time, most African-American men held only menial jobs—jobs that required few skills. Latimer would have been considered lucky if he had been able to make a living hanging wallpaper or cutting hair. He would have been considered very lucky if he had gotten to do an occasional drafting job.

Although Latimer never had the opportunity to devote full-time to the development of new inventions, he was at least able to utilize his expertise as an expert witness.

When the Civil War ended and Reconstruction began, former slaves felt a spirit of hopefulness—that at long last they would have a chance to participate in American society as full citizens. They would be able to vote, earn wages for their labor, and get a good education. Many people were disappointed when they found their efforts stifled. They found racial discrimination and other limitations on their opportunity to achieve to be discouraging. But not everyone was discouraged. Some people were lucky enough to be in the right place at the right time. Lewis Latimer's friends

Frederick Douglass and Richard Theodore Greener were such people. But even for them, good luck didn't just happen. These men were gifted in their own way. They also worked very hard to achieve their goals. When a bit of luck came their way, they were able to seize the opportunity and contribute to society at large.

The lives of most African Americans were still very bleak when Reconstruction ended in 1877. But men like Douglass, Greener, and Latimer, and such groups as the National Conference of Colored Men, continued their efforts to gain equal opportunities for everyone—regardless of race, color, or previous conditions of servitude. The three of them proved that given a chance, slaves, former slaves, and children of slaves could grow up and do great things to benefit all humankind. There were no limits to the contributions that could be made by African Americans. It was during these years that Latimer patented his most significant inventions, supervised major lighting projects in some of the largest cities in the world, wrote *the* book on lighting, and served as expert witness for Thomas Edison.

Early in the twentieth century, Latimer taught English and mechanical drawing to newly arrived immigrants at the Henry Street Settlement. World War I began; young men of all races went to fight for democracy. But when the war ended in 1918, Latimer and other civil rights advocates were disappointed that when African-American veterans got home from the war African Americans still faced obstacles that prevented them from enjoying the rights and assuming the responsibilities of citizenship. Throughout this period, Lewis Howard Latimer continued his work.

At the time of Latimer's death, William Miron Meadowcroft, historian for the Edison Pioneers, issued a statement that began: "We hardly mourn his inevitable going [death] so much as we rejoice in pleasant memory at having been associated with him in a great work for all peoples under a great man." The statement continued with a summary of Latimer's life, including his boyhood; Civil War service; drawing of the telephone patent for Alexander Graham Bell; Latimer's carbon filament invention; installing electric lights in New York, Philadelphia, and London; and his work with Edison, the Board of Patent Control, and Hammer.

Meadowcroft went on to say:

> He was of the colored race, the only one in our organization, and was one of those to respond to the initial [first] call that led to the formation of the Edison Pioneers, January 24, 1918. Broadmindedness [tolerance of many different viewpoints], versatility [the ability to use many skills] in the accomplishment of things intellectual and cultural, a linguist, a devoted husband and father, all were characteristic of him and his genial [kindly] presence will be missed from our gatherings....

The statement also told about Latimer's membership in the GAR, about his funeral and burial, and names of surviving family members. It ended with these words: "Mr. Latimer was a full member and an esteemed one, of the EDISON PIONEERS."

When the Edison Pioneers were in the process of preparing this tribute to Latimer, his daughter, Louise, wrote a letter that supplied details they did not already have. One such detail was that "Father is survived by Sister [Mrs. Gerald Norman] and myself and a sister [that is, Latimer's sister], Margaret Hawley.... She has three daughters and a son, all of whom were devoted to father." (Margaret

Lewis Latimer's sister, Margaret Hawley.

Hawley's grandchildren affectionately called their great-uncle "Uncle Lew.")

Lewis Latimer's grandchildren, Winifred and Gerald Latimer Norman, dedicated themselves to keeping his memory alive. They cooperated with such institutions as the Edison National Historic Site and such organizations as the Negro History Associates and the Unitarian Universalist Association.

In 1984, a salute to Lewis Latimer was held at the Edison National Historic Site during Black History Month. Latimer's grandchildren participated in the program. They also provided some of the materials for the exhibit organized by Marilyn Kyles, Richard Bartell, and Marjorie Taliaferro. The grandchildren were advisers to "Spike" Middleton Harris of the Negro History Associates during the production of a filmstrip on Latimer's life. They also were consultants to the Unitarian Universalist Association for a videotape and printed materials about Latimer.

Latimer's legacy of family loyalty continues from generation to generation. Not only did his grandchildren work to preserve his memory, so did the grandchildren, great-grandchildren, and great-great-grandchildren of Latimer's sister, Margaret Hawley.

The memory of Lewis Latimer is being preserved in other ways. The Henry Ford Museum in Dearborn, Michigan, has presented several exhibitions featuring Latimer. The largest was held during the mid-1970s. The highlight of this exhibit was the lighting of a Latimer lamp from the William T. Hammer Collection. The lamp was almost 100 years old at the time of the exhibition. Before this historic bulb was lit, however, many tests were made to make sure it would not be damaged in any way. The lamp proved to be as good as new! Latimer was also featured in "The Black

*Lewis Howard Latimer in a family portrait. The photograph was
taken between 1919 and 1924.*

Scientists and Inventors" traveling exhibit. This display was prepared in 1988 by the Museum of Science and Industry in Chicago.

The Queens Historical Society in Flushing, New York, also presented an exhibit on his achievements. The Latimer home in Flushing was moved about a mile from its Holly Street location to become a museum that highlights the achievements of Latimer and other African-American scientists. The Lewis H. Latimer Fund was formed to rescue the home when it was about to be torn down to make room for a housing development. The fund now raises money to preserve and maintain the home.

Each year the Latimer Achievement Awards provide college scholarships for minority students. The awards are funded by the General Electric Foundation and run by the National Society of Black Engineers. Two organizations of African-American employees honor different aspects of Latimer's contributions to science and technology. The Alliance of Black Telecommunication Employees of AT&T honor Latimer for having done the original drawings of Bell's telephone. Members of Local 3 of the Electrical Workers Union have acknowledged Latimer's contributions to the electric industry by naming their organization the Lewis H. Latimer Progressive Association. A school, a street, and a housing complex are other examples of things that have been named in Latimer's honor. In addition, in 1991, the New York Public Library's Schomburg Center for Research in Black Culture in conjunction with the Con Edison Company named a wing of their facility in honor of Lewis Howard Latimer.

Lewis Latimer was a Renaissance man in the truest sense of the term. He made himself what he was—and he had so many skills that he could honestly have said that he'd like to be remembered as draftsman, inventor, technical writer, poet, essayist, musician, linguist, artist, family man, veteran, citizen, and civil rights activist. Instead, Lewis Howard Latimer gave the definitive description of his legacy when he wrote in his journal: "I was one of the pioneers of the electric lighting industry; from its creation until it had become worldwide in its influence."

Important Dates

September 4, 1848 Lewis Latimer is born in Chelsea, Massachusetts.

1850 The Fugitive Slave Act is passed. Its provisions meant that fugitive slaves in Northern states could be taken back into slavery without a trial by jury.

1857 The Supreme Court's *Dred Scott* decision opens all federal territory to slavery and denies citizenship to African Americans.

About 1858 George Latimer leaves home. His sons are sent to a farm school; his daughter is sent to live with family friends, and Rebecca goes to sea as a stewardess.

1864 Lewis Latimer joins the Union navy. He sees action on the James River near where his parents had been slaves. His brothers, George and William, are also in the Union forces.

1865 Latimer is honorably discharged from military service. Ratification of the Thirteenth Amendment to U.S. Constitution abolishes slavery.

1868 Ratification of the Fourteenth Amendment, which states that the rights of citizenship may not be reduced or taken away.

1870 Ratification of the Fifteenth Amendment provides for equal protection of all citizens under the law.

1871–1872 Latimer is Quarter Master, Second Battalion (GAR). Latimer finds work with patent lawyers Crosby and Gould in Boston. He observes draftsman there and learns drafting.

1873 Latimer marries Mary Wilson of Fall River, Massachusetts.

1874 Latimer and W. C. Brown patent an improvement for water closets used on trains.

1876 Latimer prepares the drawings for Alexander Graham Bell's first telephone.

1879 Thomas Alva Edison invents an incandescent light bulb that uses a filament that lasts forty hours.
Lewis Latimer is out of work. He and his wife move from Boston to Bridgeport, Connecticut. There he meets Hiram S. Maxim of the U.S. Electric Lighting Company and becomes Maxim's chief draftsman.

1881 Latimer invents an improved long-burning carbon filament. Latimer and Joseph V. Nichols invent the lamp that becomes known as the "Maxim lamp." The patent is assigned to Maxim's company.
Latimer supervises the installation of lights in railroad stations, principal office buildings, and on streets in Philadelphia, New York, Montreal, and London.

1882 Latimer receives his patent for "The Process for Manufacturing Carbons."
Lewis and Mary Latimer spend part of the year in England. Latimer establishes an electrical plant and trains the English in its operation.

1883 Emma Jeanette Latimer is born.
Latimer joins the Edison Electric Light Company. He begins as special assistant to the chief counsel. Then he is a draftsman in the engineering department.

1890 Latimer writes the first book on electrical lighting. It is called *Incandescent Electric Lighting*.

Latimer becomes chief draftsman and patent expert when Edison's legal department is formed.

Louise Rebecca Latimer is born.

1894 Frederick Douglass writes Latimer about having seen his father.

Many of the legal actions of others against Edison are resolved.

Latimer has vision problems.

1896 The Board of Patent Control is formed.

1896–1906 Latimer is active in civil rights and other political concerns.

1906 Latimer teaches evening classes in English and mechanical drawing to newly arrived Eastern European immigrants at the Henry Street Settlement, New York City.

1911 The Board of Patent Control is dissolved. Latimer receives a pension.

Latimer joins Edwin Hammer's firm as an electrical engineer.

1918 The Edison Pioneers is formed. Latimer is a charter member.

1924 Mary Wilson Latimer dies.

Latimer retires from Hammer & Schwarz.

1925 Latimer's family and friends privately publish his *Poems of Love and Life*.

December 11, 1928 Lewis Howard Latimer dies.

Bibliography

Books

Baker, Henry E. *The Colored Inventor*. New York: Crises Publishing Co., 1913. Reprint. New York: 1969.

Blassingame, John W. *Frederick Douglass*: *The Clarion Voice*. Washington, D.C.: National Park Service Division of Publications, 1969.

1863 Boston City Directory. Boston: Adams, Sampson and Company, 1863.

1864 Boston City Directory. Boston: Adams, Sampson and Co., 1864.

1868 Boston City Directory. Boston: Sampson, Davenport and Co., 1868.

1870 Boston City Directory. Boston: Sampson, Davenport, 1870.

1874 Boston City Directory. Boston: Sampson, Davenport and Co., 1874.

1876 Boston City Directory. Boston: Sampson, Davenport and Co., 1876.

1877 Boston City Directory. Boston: Sampson, Davenport and Co., 1877.

Burckel, Christian E. *Who's Who in Colored America; An Illustrated Biographical Directory of Notable Living Persons of African Descent in the United States.* 7 vols. Yonkers, New York, 1927–50.

Burt, McKinley. *Black Inventors of America.* Portland, Oregon: National Book Company, 1969.

Diggs, Irene. *Black Innovators.* Chicago: Institute of Positive Education, 1975.

Dyer, Frank Lewis, and Thomas Commerford Martin. *Edison: His Life and Inventions.* New York: Harper and Brothers, 1910.

Haber Louis. *Black Pioneers of Science and Invention.* New York: Harcourt, Brace and World, 1970.

Harris, Middleton, et al. *The Black Book.* New York: Random House, 1974.

Hayden, Robert C. *Eight Black American Inventors.* Reading, Massachusetts: Addison-Wesley, 1972.

Herkimer, Herbert. *The Engineer's Illustrated Thesaurus.* New York: Chemical Publishing Co., 1952.

Hutchinson, John Wallace. *Story of the Hutchinsons.* Boston: Lee and Shepard Publishers, 1896.

Ives, Patricia Carter. *Creativity and Inventions.* Arlington, Virginia: Research Unlimited, 1987.

Jehl, Francis. *Menlo Park.* Vol. 2–3. Dearborn, Michigan: The Edison Institute, 1941.

Kirkham, E.K. *A Handy Guide to Record Searching in the Larger Cities of the United States.* Logan, Utah: Everton Publishers, n.d.

Latimer, Lewis Howard. *Poems of Love and Life*. New York: Friends and Admirers of His Seventy-Seventh Birthday, 1925.

Latimer, Lewis Howard. *Incandescent Electric Lighting*. New York: D. Van Nostrand Co., 1890.

Lewis, Floyd A. *The Incandescent Light*. Foreword by Charles F. Kettering. West Orange, New Jersey: The Thomas Alva Edison Foundation, Inc., 1949.

Logan, Rayford, and Michael R. Winston, eds. *Directory of American Negro Biography*. New York: W.W Norton, 1982.

1875 Lynn City Directory. Boston: Sampson, Davenport and Co., 1875.

Ploski, Harry A., and James Williams. *The Negro Almanac: A Reference Work on the African American*. Detroit: Gale Research, Inc., 1989.

Rush, Theressa Gunnels. *Black American Writers Past and Present*. Metuchen, New Jersey: Scarecrow Press, 1975.

U.S. Department of Energy. *Black Contributors to Science and Energy Technology*. Washington, D.C.: United States Government Printing Office, 1979.

Urdang, Laurence, ed. *Timetables of American History*. Introduction by Henry Steele Commager. New York: Simon and Schuster, 1981.

Van Sertima, Ivan, ed. *Blacks in Science: Ancient and Modern*. *John Henrik Clarke*. "Lewis Howard Latimer." New Brunswick, New Jersey: Transaction Press, 1983.

Wesley, Charles. *International Library of Negro Life and History*. *The Quest for Equality*. New York: Publishers Company, Inc., 1969.

Williams, James C. *At Last Recognition in America.* Vol. 1. Chicago: BCA Publishing Corp., 1978.

Winslow, Eugene, ed. *Black Americans in Science and Engineering.* Chicago: Afro-Am Publishing Co., 1974.

Newspapers and Journals

Davis, Asa J. "Two Autobiographical Fragments of George W. Latimer (1820–1896): A Preliminary Assessment," *Journal of Afro-American Historical and Genealogical Society.* 1 (1980): 3–18.

"Effort to Save a Site and Light Up a Life." *New York Times,* 8 August 1988, p. 28.

"Grandchildren of Invention." *The World: Journal of the Unitarian Universalist Association.* Vol. 3, no. 1 (January/February 1989).

Ives, Patricia Carter. "Patent and Trademark Innovations of Black Americans and Women." *Journal of the Patent Office Society.* Vol. 62, no. 2 (February 1980): 108–19.

Unpublished Materials

Alexander Graham Bell Papers. Library of Congress, Washington, D.C.

John E. Bruce Collection. Schomburg Center for Research in Black Culture of the New York Public Library, New York.

Edison Pioneers Archival Files. Edison National Historic Site, West Orange, New Jersey.

Thomas Alva Edison Collection. Archives, Henry Ford Museum and Greenfield Village, Dearborn, Michigan.

G.A.R. [Grand Army of the Republic] Papers. Chicago Public Library, Chicago, Illinois.

Lewis H. Latimer Papers. Schomburg Center for Research in Black Culture of the New York Public Library, New York.

Middleton "Spike" Harris Collection. Schomburg Center for Research in Black Culture of the New York Public Library, New York.

Interviews

Mr. Bande'le. Latimer/Woods economic organization founded by Assemblyman Roger Green, Brooklyn. 7 January 1988. (By telephone)

Bartell, Richard. Teacher and graduate history student of Dr. Price at Rutgers University. Particularly interested in Latimer and black participation in the Civil War. 1988. (By telephone)

Bockman, Eugene J. Commissioner for New York City Department of Records and Information Services. 17 January 1988. (By telephone)

Brandon, George. Professor at University of Maryland who organized an exhibit of black scientists. 7 June 1988. (By telephone)

Brigham, Florence. Fall River Historical Society, Fall River River, Massachusetts. 3, 4, and 11 August 1990. (By telephone)

Cascome, Jeanette. Association for the Study of African American Life and History, Roselle, New Jersey. 30 September 1988.

Chamura, John. National Archives, New York Branch, Bayonne, New Jersey. 8 January 1988. (By telephone)

Davis, Asa. Professor of History and Black Studies at Amherst College, Amherst, Massachusetts. 12 June 1988 (by telephone) and 8 May 1990 (in person).

Greenleaf, Fay. Administrative assistant, Lynn Historical Society, Lynn, Massachusetts. 2, 3, 4, and 8 August 1990. (By telephone)

Hayden, Carla. School of Library Science, University of Pittsburgh, Pittsburgh, Pennsylvania. Formerly director of the Children's Science Library at the Museum of Science and Industry in Chicago. 9 September 1987.

Ives, Patricia Carter. Technical adviser for the U.S. Patent and Trademark videotape *From Dreams to Reality*; patent examiner, Chemical Division of the U.S. Patent and Trademark Office; historian and genealogist. 3 March 1988, 27 December 1988, 3 April 1989. (By telephone)

Koolakian, Robert G. Latimer family friend formerly on staff at Greenfield Village in Dearborn, Michigan. Syracuse, New York. 9 September 1988. (By telephone)

Kyles, Marilyn. Museum technician (registrar), Edison National Historic Site. Four interviews in person and numerous phone consultations during course of research and writing.

Lachatanere, Diana. Head, Rare Books, Manuscripts, and Archives Section, Schomburg Center for Research in Black Culture, New York Public Library.

Ludder, Henry. Queens Borough Hall, Queens, New York. 17 July 1988. (By telephone)

Medeiros, Denise. Librarian, Fall River Public Library, Fall River, Massachusetts. 2, 3 August 1990. (By telephone)

Mrozinski, Mary. Executive Director, Queens Historical Society, Flushing, New York. 10 August 1988. (By telephone)

Norman, Winifred Latimer. Granddaughter of Lewis Howard Latimer, New York. Telephone interviews 4 August 1987, 15 October 1987, 27 April 1988, 7 July 1988, 11 August 1988, 13 September 1988, 30 March 1989, 6 August 1990. In-person interviews 25 August 1987 and 20 July 1988.

Wallace, William, IV. Executive Director of Latimer/Woods Foundation, New York. 2 February 1988.

Woodtar, Dee. African-American history specialist, Newberry Library, Chicago, Illinois. 14 November 1989, 5–8 May 1990, and 31 July 1990.

Wright, Giles. New Jersey State Historical Society. 8 January 1988. (By telephone)

Yearwood, Mary. Rare Books, Manuscripts, and Archives Section, Schomburg Center for Research in Black Culture of the New York Public Library. 8 January 1988 and 2 February 1988.

Zepp, Eugene. Librarian, Rare Books Division, Boston Public Library, Boston, Massachusetts. 3 August 1990. (By telephone)

Phone conversation with researcher at American Military Institute, Washington, D.C. 4 March 1988.

Phone conversation with researcher at Chicago Municipal Records Library, Chicago, Illinois. 4 April 1988.

Phone conversation with secretary at Oak Grove Cemetery, Fall River, Massachusetts. 9 October 1988 and 3 August 1990.

Phone conversation with researcher at SCIPIO Society of Naval and Military History, Cold Spring Harbor, New York. 3 April 1988.

Phone conversation with Branch Chief, Legislative, Judicial, and Fiscal Branch of the National Archives, Civil Archives Division, Washington, D.C. 9 July 1988.

Phone conversation with librarian, New York State Historical Association, Cooperstown, New York. 11 February 1988.

Index

Acknowledgments

ACKNOWLEDGMENTS:

Special thanks to Dr. Asa Davis; Dr. Addie Harris; Archives Department of the Edison National Historic Site; Schomburg Center for Research in Black Culture of the New York Public Library; Archives & Library, Henry Ford Museum; Massachusetts Historical Society; Boston Public Library; Mr. Eugene Zepp; Fall River Historical Library; Mrs. Florence Brigham, Fall River Public Library; Mrs. Denise Medeiros; Queens Historical Society; Mr. Robert G. Koolakian; Rev. Robert M. Helmstreet; Unitarian Universalist Church of Flushing, N.Y.; Unitarian Universalist Association; Mrs. Fay Greenleaf; Lynn Historical Society; Greenfield Village; Wheaton Public Library; Ms. Nelva Hamlin; Mrs. Ursula Ulrich; Mr. Werner Ulrich; Mr. Albert Turner, Mrs. Patricia Carter Ives; Ms. Bess Rupert; Ms. Jorie Wilcox; Dr. Dee Woodtar; Newberry Library; National Archives; Dr. Sylvia Cooke Martin; Library of Congress; DuSable Museum of African American History; Mrs. Ida Mae Cress; Night Owl Library Service; Chicago Public Library; Dr. John Henrik Clarke; Dr. John G. Jackson; Mrs. Darwin Walton; and Ms. Jacqueline McQueen.

PHOTOGRAPH CREDITS:

Culver Pictures: p. 14; Massachusetts Historical Society: p. 12; Collection of Winifred Latimer Norman, photos by John Lei: pp. 38, 55, 84, 96; The Schomburg Center for Research in Black Culture, The New York Public Library, Astor, Lenox and Tilden Foundations: pp. 28, 43, 64–65, 67, 72, 90, 102; U.S. Department of the Interior, National Park Service, Edison National Historic Site: pp. 50, 58–59, 92–93, 104–105.

TEXT PERMISSIONS:

Permissions granted by Miss Winifred Norman for reprinting Lewis Howard Latimer's poems "Friends" and "Ebon Venus" and excerpts from his personal journal and correspondence; the Schomburg Center for Research in Black Culture of the New York Public Library for reprinting excerpts from Mrs. Mary Wilson Latimer's personal journal; and the Edison National Historic Site for reprinting excerpts from the "Tribute from the Edison Pioneers" and *The Incandescent Light;* the Massachusetts Historical Society for reprinting excerpts of the *Latimer Journal.*

About the Author

Glennette Tilley Turner is an author, educator, and historian who lives with her husband in Wheaton, Illinois. *Lewis Howard Latimer* is her fourth book and second biography. The first biography is the best-selling *Take a Walk in Their Shoes*, a collective biography with skits. Her articles or stories have appeared in such publications as Open Court Readers, *Scholastic Scope, Ebony, Jr!*, and *Encore* magazines, and the *Chicago Tribune*.

For nearly twenty-five years Turner was an elementary teacher. Prior to her recent retirement, she was named Outstanding Woman Educator in DuPage County, Illinois. She continues in the educational field as student teacher evaluator at National Louis University.

Her bachelor's degree is in English from Lake Forest College, and her master's degree from Goddard College is in History and Juvenile Literature. She is former president of Children's Reading Roundtable of Chicago and of the Black Literary Umbrella.

Turner has done extensive research on the Underground Railroad, and has great interest in oral history. She often writes and speaks on both topics.